Constitutional Law in Ireland

Constitutional Law in Ireland

Laura Cahillane
Seán ó Conaill

This book was originally published as a monograph in the International Encyclopaedia of Laws/Constitutional Law.

Founding Editor: Roger Blanpain
General Editor: Frank Hendrickx
Volume Editors: André Alen & David Haljan

Wolters Kluwer

Published by:
Kluwer Law International B.V.
PO Box 316
2400 AH Alphen aan den Rijn
The Netherlands
Website: www.wolterskluwerlr.com

Sold and distributed in North, Central and South America by:
Wolters Kluwer Legal & Regulatory U.S.
7201 McKinney Circle
Frederick, MD 21704
United States of America
Email: customer.service@wolterskluwer.com

Sold and distributed in all other countries by:
Quadrant
Rockwood House
Haywards Heath
West Sussex
RH16 3DH
United Kingdom
Email: international-customerservice@wolterskluwer.com

ISBN 978-90-411-9309-4

e-Book: ISBN 978-90-411-9341-4
web-PDF: ISBN 978-90-411-9373-5

This title is available on www.kluwerlawonline.com

The Authors

Dr Laura Cahillane is a lecturer in the School of Law, University of Limerick. She is a first class honours graduate of University College Cork (BCL (Law and French) 2007, LLM (by Research) 2008, PhD 2012, PGCTHLE 2013). Laura undertook a Post-Doctoral Fellowship in UCC and held lectureships in UCC and DCU before joining the School of Law at UL. Her research interests lie in the areas of Constitutional Law, Legal History, Judicial Politics and Comparative Law and she has published nationally and internationally in these areas. She is the author of *Drafting the Irish Free State Constitution* (MUP 2016).

Dr Seán Ó Conaill is a lecturer in Law and Irish at the School of Law, University College Cork. He is a graduate of University College Cork (BCL (Law and Irish) 2005, LLM (Criminal Justice) 2007) and Cardiff University (PhD 2013). Prior to joining the School of Law at UCC Seán held a teaching fellowship at the School of Welsh at Cardiff University. His research interests lie in the areas of Constitutional Law, the

The Authors

Irish Language, Language Law and Sports Law and he has published through the medium of both English and Irish languages in these areas.

Table of Contents

Table of Contents

List of Abbreviations

ECHR	European Convention on Human Rights
ECtHR	European Court of Human Rights
ICC	International Criminal Court
IRA	Irish Republican Army
JAAB	Judicial Appointments Advisory Board
NATO	North Atlantic Treaty Organization
PR-STV	Proportional Representation with the Single Transferable Vote
RTE	Raidió Teilifís Éireann

Explanation of Terms

Brehon Law	Ancient Celtic law of Ireland
Bunreacht na hÉireann	The Irish Basic Law/Constitution
Ceann comhairle	Chairperson of the Dáil
Dáil Éireann	Lower House of Parliament
Éire	Irish word for Ireland
Gardaí	Police force operating in Ireland
Oireachtas	Irish Parliament
Saorstát Éireann	The Irish Free State
Seanad Cathaoirleach	Chairperson of the Seanad
Seanad Éireann	Senate – Upper House of Parliament
Tánaiste	Deputy Prime Minister of Ireland
Taoiseach	Prime Minister
Teachtaí Dála (TD)	Member of the Irish parliament- Dáil Éireann

General Introduction

§1. An Outline of Irish Constitutional History

1. The Modern Irish State came into being on 6 December 1922 after the Irish and British Parliaments had passed an Act bringing the Irish Free State Constitution in to force.[1] However, in order to understand the context behind Ireland's constitutional history it is necessary to briefly explain the various developments which led up to this point.

2. Before the arrival of the English, Ireland had a native system of law known as the '*Brehon Law*' which was based primarily on custom. It was administered by travelling figures known as '*Brehons*', sometimes compared to travelling justices. The Common Law was brought to Ireland following the Anglo-Norman invasion in 1169. It took many years to conquer the whole island but by the seventeenth century, the English conquest was complete and the English Common Law system was firmly embedded. At this time, there was an Irish Parliament but the British Westminster Parliament had ultimate control. There was a brief restoration of Irish Parliamentary autonomy in 1782 when the Westminster Parliament amended Poynings' Act and renounced its claim to legislate for Ireland.[2] This period, known as 'Grattan's Parliament' did not last long and in 1800, Westminster finally put an end to the separate Irish Parliament with The Acts of Union. From then until 1921, Ireland was governed from London; a situation which was not acceptable to many Irish people and many unsuccessful rebellions and uprisings took place.

3. The early twentieth century saw developments in the fight for Home Rule. Following the veto of two previous Bills by the House of Lords, in 1911 the power of that House to veto bills was substituted with a two-year delay and so in 1912, a final Home Rule Bill was passed and was due to become law in 1914. However, the outbreak of World War I meant that the Bill could not be put into operation and eventually, it was overtaken by other events. During Easter 1916, another unsuccessful rising took place in Ireland. However, due to the brutal actions taken by the British in suppressing the Rising and executing the leaders following trials by field general court martial, the

1. There is a disagreement as to whether the British or the Irish Act is the original source of authority but the Irish Courts have declared the Irish Act as the original source. *See State (Ryan) v. Lennon* [1935] IR 170, 203. For more on the differing interpretations of both sides, *see* Thomas Mohr, 'Law Without Loyalty – The Abolition of the Irish Appeal to the Privy Council' (2002) Irish Jurist 187.
2. Poynings' Act refers to a series of statutes enacted by Poynings' Parliament from 1494-5, two chapters of which gave legislative power over Ireland to England. It was first amended in 1782 and later repealed in 1878.

Irish public became sympathetic to the ideals behind the 1916 Rising and eventually this culminated in the War of Independence, which began in 1919. This was the same year that the Irish Parliament, *Dáil Éireann*, was constituted. The elected representatives of the *Sinn Féin* Party, (which was credited with the Rising, and which had overtaken the old Irish Parliamentary Party as the largest party in Ireland in the general election of 1918), refused to take their seats in Westminster and instead met in Dublin and established *Dáil Éireann*, a body which was not recognized by Britain. Later, a version of the original 1912 Act was passed and became The Government of Ireland Act 1920. However, this was regarded as too little too late and was no longer acceptable to the Irish, who now fought for independence rather than Home Rule.

4. Guerrilla warfare continued until a truce was agreed in 1921. Following this, the Anglo-Irish Treaty was signed, the result of which meant that the twenty-six counties (now known as the Republic of Ireland) became the 'Irish Free State' and had dominion status[3] with the remaining six counties of Northern Ireland opting to remain within the United Kingdom.[4] The signing of the Treaty finally gave Ireland independence; while the State would remain in the British Commonwealth, it finally had control over its own affairs. However, the Treaty settlement did not please everyone and some believed that Ireland should have held out for 'complete independence' which would have severed all ties with Britain. The settlement which had been agreed made certain concessions, including the fact that Irish members of Parliament had to swear an oath of faithfulness to the King, something which was anathema to many Irish people. Disputes arose during the vote on the Treaty in the *Dáil* and when the 'anti-Treaty' side lost the crucial vote, these Deputies walked out of Parliament and refused to take their seats. This culminated in a bitter Civil War which lasted for almost a year and was eventually put down by Free State forces. By the 1930s, the Anti-Treaty side had decided that they would take their seats in Parliament but on the grounds that they would take the oath as an 'empty formula'. Eventually this, along with many other undesirable British relics was eventually removed from the Constitution.

I. The Irish Free State Constitution

5. As part of the 1921 settlement, it was agreed that the Irish would draft their own constitution. This task was overseen by the two leaders of the Pro-Treaty side: Michael Collins and Arthur Griffith. They gathered a committee of nine men of differing backgrounds, including five lawyers, a writer, a businessman, a professor and a civil servant. This committee produced three potential drafts of a constitution after only six weeks of study and discussions. A suitable draft was chosen and was then brought to London for discussion. The decision to bring the draft to London before laying it before

3. In a pronouncement made during the Imperial Conference of 1926 Great Britain and the dominions were described as 'autonomous communities within the British Empire, equal in status, in no way subordinate one to another in any aspect of their domestic or external affairs, though united by a common allegiance to the Crown and freely associated as members of the British Commonwealth of Nations.'
4. Article 12 of the Treaty envisaged an all-Ireland arrangement but provided for an opt-out clause for Northern Ireland, which was taken up.

the Irish Constituent Assembly was a controversial one but with the benefit of hindsight we can say it was a necessary one. Since the Constitution would also have to pass through the Westminster Parliament, it was important that the draft was acceptable to the British. Unfortunately for the Irish delegation, the British were furious with the draft, which they felt was an abrogation of the Treaty and an attempt to create 'a republic in disguise', a response which meant days of frantic renegotiations and redrafting.

6. Eventually, a draft emerged which pleased the British. However, this draft now contained many British symbols and features which, while they were all essentially theoretical and had no real practical significance, would be unacceptable to the Anti-Treaty side. It had been hoped that the impasse in the Treaty disagreement could be broken by a Constitution which demonstrated de facto Irish independence but the insistence by the British on the inclusion of the oath, amongst other similar provisions, dashed all hopes of reconciliation.

7. The Constitution was passed through the Irish and British Parliaments and came into force on 6 December 1922 and while it now looked more like the Constitution of a Dominion, it had retained the essential features which had been drafted by the Irish Committee. The central themes which shone through the document were the related ideas of popular sovereignty and democracy. Popular sovereignty was a feature which the Irish felt was imperative to the Constitution and which they insisted on retaining during the British negotiations. This was because it was felt that in order for the ordinary Irish people to accept and embrace the new constitutional order, it had to be proven to them that this was, in fact, their Constitution. Following years of oppression and British rule, many people were distrustful of politics and the State, so proclaiming at the beginning of the Constitution that the people, rather than any organ of State, was sovereign, was crucial. There were various devices included in the Constitution in order to further this agenda: the referendum was included for constitutional amendments and as a potential legislative veto; the initiative procedure to allow the people to propose their own laws and constitutional amendments was provided for; a bicameral legislature was created (with a second House to represent minority interests); the executive was to include external expert ministers to run particular departments; the Government was made responsible to the lower House, the *Dáil*; a distinct separation of powers was created and the High Court was given the power of judicial review.

8. However, while all of these features were intended to further the goals of popular sovereignty and democracy, Civil War politics intervened and many of the provisions were either misused or removed entirely from the Constitution. This process was accelerated by a small change to the amendment provision before the Constitution was promulgated. While the referendum was the only method originally specified for amendments to the Constitution, it was noted in the Constituent Assembly that minor changes might be needed to resolve teething problems that might arise once the Constitution was in operation and it would be costly to run a referendum for the purpose of addressing these minor sorts of changes. Therefore it was decided that for the first eight years, amendments could be made by ordinary legislation. However, it was never specified that this process was purely for minor changes, and that the provision itself could not be amended. The result was that the referendum was by-passed by the various Governments who abused this particular power and amended the original time-limit to provide for potentially endless amendments by those in control of the lower House of Parliament. Due to the various amendments which had taken place by the mid-1930s, it was recognized that the Constitution was now 'a thing of shreds and patches' and it was decided to create a new Constitution.[5]

II. The Need for a New Constitution

9. In 1926, the leader of the Anti-Treaty side, Eamon de Valera, formed a new political party called '*Fianna Fáil*' and decided to re-enter parliamentary politics. The party entered the *Dáil* in 1927, despite the fact that in order to do so, the Deputies had to swear the oath of faithfulness to the King, which was the ultimate cause of the split in the first place. However, members of *Fianna Fáil* declared that they saw the oath as an 'empty formula' and took it only on that basis. *Fianna Fáil* entered Government in 1932, at which point de Valera began in earnest his plan to dismantle any remaining imperial ties in the Constitution. He introduced a Bill to abolish the oath in 1932 and later abolished the office of Governor-General, which had previously represented the British monarch in Ireland, and deleted all references to the King. By 1936, the Constitution was now excised of the controversial symbols and references which had caused so much turmoil in 1922. However, the Constitution was ravaged, having been amended twenty-five times; some were minor amendments, some were to advance de Valera's goal of purging the Constitution of the imperial elements, while others were casualties of Civil War politics, such as the removal of the referendum and initiative.[6] Since 1934 however, de Valera had been working on formulating a draft for a new Constitution.

10. In 1934, four senior civil servants were given the task of reviewing the existing Constitution. Their report suggested retaining much of the Constitution but adding some innovations. The official drafting of a new Constitution then began in 1935 with de Valera providing instructions to John Hearne, Legal Adviser in the Department of External Affairs, who would later become the principal drafter. Unlike its predecessor, which was translated into Irish only after the English version was agreed upon, the new Constitution, *Bunreacht na hÉireann*, was drafted in both languages. While Hearne was the architect of the English version, Micheál Ó Gríobhtha was given the task of drafting the Irish version. This meant that in the end, some of the successful provisions which ended up in the Constitution were drawn from both the original English and Irish versions. This has caused some anomalies where the two texts do not translate exactly. In order to avoid these difficulties, it was decided that the Irish version would take precedence in case of conflict. This decision was

5. For more on the 1922 Constitution *see* Laura Cahillane, *Drafting the Irish Free State Constitution* (MUP 2016).

6. These devices were taken out of the Constitution in 1928 without ever having been used because the Government was fearful of de Valera's plan to use the initiative to remove the parliamentary oath from the Constitution, something which would not have been welcome by the British Government at the time.

made more for nationalistic reasons concerned with the preservation and status of Irish rather than for any legal or technical reason.[7]

11. Various groups were consulted during the drafting period, the Catholic Church being the most influential. While the influence of the Church has, at times, been exaggerated, John Charles McQuaid, future Archbishop of Dublin did indeed play a prominent role, providing suggestions, drafts and instructions. However, recent scholarship has demonstrated that while the influence of the Catholic Church was significant, it did not dictate terms entirely. In fact de Valera's reluctance to accept some of the more religious aspects caused some tension.[8] The Constitution was approved by the *Dáil* in June of 1937 and was narrowly approved by the people in a referendum in July of that year.

III. Bunreacht na hÉireann

12. While the decision was taken to create an entirely new Constitution, much of the original 1922 document was actually retained, so much so that the new Constitution was described as 'a re-bottling of wine most of which was by then quite old and of familiar vintages'.[9] Certain changes and innovations were brought to the new document though. The most obvious change concerned structure; where before the fundamental rights provisions appeared at the beginning, immediately after the provisions describing the State, they now appear at the end of the document. This section was also strengthened substantially, with rights being added to sections on the family, education and property. While the 1922 Constitution declared at the beginning that the Irish Free State was a member of the British Commonwealth, the new Constitution declares that the name of the State is *Éire*, or in the English language, Ireland,[10] and conveniently, did not mention the fact that the State was still technically a member of the British Commonwealth.[11] The new Constitution also created the office of a popularly elected President as head of State in place of the previously unelected office of the Governor General. The tone of the new Constitution is also quite religious, in stark contrast to its predecessor, in which God was not mentioned.[12] Bunreacht na hÉireann begins with a reference to 'the Most Holy Trinity, from whom is all authority ...' and many more such references

7. *See* further Part V Chapter 5.
8. *See* John Henry Whyte, *Church and State in Modern Ireland 1923-1979* (2nd edn Gill & Macmillan Dublin 1980); Gerard Hogan, 'Law and Religion: Church-State Relations in Ireland from Independence to the Present Day' (1987) 35 AJCL 47; Dermot Keogh, 'The Constitutional Revolution: An Analysis of the Making of the Constitution' in Frank Litton (ed.) *The Constitution of Ireland 1937- 1987* (Institute of Public Administration Dublin 1988) 50; Dermot Keogh, *Ireland and the Vatican: the politics and diplomacy of church-state relations, 1922-1960* (Cork University Press 1995) p xxi.
9. *See* Gerard Hogan and Gerard Whyte *JM Kelly: The Irish Constitution* (Butterworths Dublin 2003), preface to the first edition.
10. *See* more on the name at para. 64.
11. Now referred to simply as the Commonwealth, this is an association of States, most of which are former British colonies and continue to recognize the Queen as their monarch.
12. God was mentioned in the preamble to the Constituent Act.

appear throughout the document. The new Constitution is also much longer and more detailed than the 1922 document with language that is, at times, more complicated.

§2. CHARACTERISTICS OF THE IRISH STATE

13. The Irish State is still a relatively young State, having achieved independence in 1922. At that stage, the six counties in the North of Ireland opted to remain part of the United Kingdom while the twenty-six counties of what is now known as the Republic of Ireland became an independent State.

14. Article 5 of Bunreacht na hÉireann declares that Ireland is a sovereign, independent, democratic State. Article 6 states further that: 'All powers of government, legislative, executive and judicial, derive, under God, from the people, whose right it is to designate the rulers of the State and, in final appeal, to decide all questions of national policy, according to the requirements of the common good.' By this Article, it is accepted that the Constitution embraces the separation of powers doctrine and envisages separate branches of government for the executive, legislative and judicial functions. While, this is true in theory, the reality is that Ireland has a fused executive-legislature due to the way in which the political system works in Ireland.[13] However, the judicial branch is separate from the executive and legislature.

15. Article 6 also emphasizes the principle of popular sovereignty. The case of *Byrne v. Ireland*[14] confirmed that the State is the creation of the People on the basis of this Article, in conjunction with Article 1, which declares that 'The Irish nation affirms its ... sovereign right to choose its own form of Government' and Articles 46 and 47 which underline the importance of the people in amending the Constitution. The terms People, Nation and State are all referred to in the Constitution and while earlier analysis might have construed the State as the body which 'represents and incorporates the People',[15] the *Byrne* case decided that the State is subordinate to and separate from the People. In *Crotty v. An Taoiseach*,[16] it was recognized that the People are the guardians of the Constitution and in *Hanafin v. Minister for the Environment*,[17] it was confirmed that the organs of State are not entitled to interfere with the will of the People, as expressed by a referendum vote and that it is the right of the People to decide all questions of national policy by way of the referendum process. The term Nation is not always used consistently within the document: at times it is used as a synonym for 'State', whereas at other times 'Nation' and 'State' are clearly distinct. Forde has interpreted the word 'Nation' in the Constitution as embracing 'Irish people living anywhere, whether in Northern Ireland or perhaps also abroad'.[18]

16. The legal personality of the State is not mentioned in the Constitution but as a result of a number of cases, we can say that the State is a juristic person and can

13. *See* more at paras 68–72 and 95 et seq.
14. [1972] IR 241.
15. David Morgan, *Constitutional Law of Ireland* (2nd edn, Roundhall 1990) 28.
16. [1987] IR 713.
17. [1996] 3 IR 321.
18. Michael Forde and D avid Leonard, *Constitutional Law of Ireland*, (3rd edn, Bloomsbury, 2013) 59.

own property and enter into contracts in its own right,[19] it is capable of enjoying rights[20] and is obliged to protect the rights of citizens,[21] the State can be sued[22] and can sue other persons.[23]

17. While the State is defined as 'independent' in Article 5, this is qualified by Article 29.4.6° and Ireland's membership of the European Union.[24]

§3. State Territory, Population and Demographics

18. 'Ireland' refers to the twenty-six counties of the Republic of Ireland. The remaining six counties of Northern Ireland are part of the United Kingdom. The entire island of Ireland covers 84,415 sq. km and out of this, the Republic of Ireland covers 70,283 sq. km.[25]

According to the most recent census data, obtained in 2016, the population of Ireland is 4,757,976. In 2011, according to the previous census, the figure was 4,588,252. While a breakdown is not yet available on the 2016 figures, in 2011, 3,831,187 respondents classified themselves as Roman Catholic, 124,445 classified themselves as Church of Ireland (or England, Anglican, Episcopalian), while 256,83 entered no religion at all, the remaining religious denominations included Muslims, Orthodox Christians (Greek, Coptic, Russian), Presbyterians, Apostolics, and other Christian and religious sects.

19. *Comyn v. Attorney General* [1950] IR 142.
20. *Osheku v. Ireland* [1986] IR 733.
21. *Cox v. Ireland* [1992] 2 IR 503.
22. *Byrne* (n. 14).
23. *Comyn* (n. 19) *supra* .
24. *See* more at paras 21–22.
25. Ordnance Survey of Ireland.

Part I. Sources of Constitutional Law

Chapter 1. Treaties

§1. Treaty Making Power

19. According to Article 29.4, the power to commit the State to an international agreement is vested in the Government, since the Article declares that 'the executive power of the State in connection with its external relations shall ... be exercised by ... the Government.' However, for so-called head of State agreements, the President executes treaties on behalf of the State. While the President is named as a contracting party, he will be represented by a plenipotentiary.[26]

Article 29.5 declares that every international agreement to which the State becomes a party, except those of a technical and administrative character must also be laid before the *Dáil*. It further specifies that the State shall not be bound by any international agreement involving a charge upon public funds unless its terms have been approved by the *Dáil*. The practice is that the Government will enter into an international agreement and the agreement will then be laid before the *Dáil*. It was decided in the case of *Hutchinson v. Minister for Justice*[27] that this only applies in respect of agreements which have already been ratified by the State.

§2. Dualism

20. Ireland is a dualist State, as is made clear by Article 29.6 which states that no international agreement can be made part of domestic law unless it has been incorporated into Irish law by the *Oireachtas*. Thus, while the State may sign up to international agreements, unless they have been approved and passed through the *Oireachtas*, they cannot be relied upon in the Irish Courts.

26. Hogan and Whyte, *JM Kelly: The Irish Constitution* (n. 9) 508.
27. [1993] 3 IR 567.

§3. Treaties of the European Union

21. There is one significant exception to the principle of dualism in Ireland; Article 29.4.6° sets out a separate procedure for relations with the European Union. This provision was inserted into the Constitution to allow Ireland to join the European Communities, along with the UK and Denmark, in 1973. The Article prevents the possibility of any constitutional challenge to 'laws enacted, acts done or measures adopted' by the EU by providing that nothing in the Constitution shall prevent these laws or acts, which are necessitated by the obligations of membership, from having force of law in the State. This provision, in conjunction with the EU law principle of 'Supremacy', means that in the case of a conflict between an aspect of EU law and the Irish Constitution, the law of the EU must prevail.

22. While this Article provides a very strong basis for EU law in the Irish Constitution, questions subsequently arose as to whether a further amendment was needed when the scope and objectives of the original body, the European Communities, began to change. This was considered in the case of *Crotty v. An Taoiseach*,[28] where Finlay CJ pointed out that the European Communities were dynamic in nature and therefore must be expected to develop and change. He also held that the amendment inserted in 1973 which allowed Ireland to join this Community also authorized the State to join in amendments of the founding treaties, without a further amendment to the Constitution, so long as the essential scope of objectives of the Community remains the same. However, if the changes to the founding treaties were outside of the broad purpose and objectives, as originally envisaged in 1973, they will not be covered by Article 29.4. 6° and a further referendum will be required to amend the Constitution accordingly. This has led to a number of referendums in recent years in Ireland, the most notable being the Nice and Lisbon Treaty referendums, both of which were originally rejected by the Irish people but following re-negotiation and subsequent referendums, both Treaties were eventually approved. Their rejection would have meant that the Treaties could not have been ratified by the EU.

28. *Crotty* (n. 16).

Chapter 2. The Constitution

§1. Introduction

23. As we have already seen in the section on Constitutional History, the current Constitution is Bunreacht na hÉireann, which replaced the 1922 Irish Free State Constitution in 1937. It was enacted by the Irish people after a plebiscite and was passed by a majority of 158,160 votes. It is written in both English and Irish. Both versions were drawn up independently and are not direct translations of each other.[29] In cases of conflict between both languages, the Irish version will take precedence. The Irish title, translated into English, means basic law of Ireland.

24. The Constitution contains fifty articles, which are further divided into sections and subsections. Most articles are drafted quite broadly and the meaning of these articles has been interpreted by the superior courts through case law.

25. The Constitution has been described as both 'law and manifesto' since it contains not just the basic legal principles, rules and structure of the organs of State but also what are referred to as 'aspirations'.[30] The Constitution originally contained some controversial aspirations; the original Articles 2 and 3, for example, declared that the 'national territory' of Ireland included the whole island of Ireland. This was amended in 1998 as part of the Good Friday Agreement.[31] Another amendment in 1972 removed the 'special position' of the Roman Catholic Church from Article 44. However, the Constitution still contains much religious language, most notably in the Preamble. This remains a somewhat controversial aspect of the Constitution along with a few further provisions, such as Article 41 on the family, which also provides that women should not be required to 'engage in labour to the neglect of their duties in the home'. This is one provision which can be regarded as an antiquated product of its time and it has been earmarked for reform.

26. The Constitution also sets out the basic framework of government and contains details on the workings and relationships between the various organs of State. Article 6 declares that all powers of government derive under God from the people.

---

29. *See* All-Party Oireachtas Committee on the Constitution, *Bunreacht na hÉireann: A Study of the Irish text* (Stationery Office, 1999); M Cearúil, *Bunreacht na hÉireann: a Study of the Irish text* (Dublin, The Stationery Office, 1999).

30. John Maurice Kelly, 'The Constitution: Law and Manifesto', in Frank Litton (ed) *The Constitution of Ireland 1937-87* (1988) 208, citing the Supreme Court in *Re the Criminal Law (Jurisdiction) Bill 1975* [1977] IR 129.

31. Six counties in the North of Ireland are not part of the Irish State but opted to remain within the United Kingdom when the Irish Free State was created. This created tension over the years which culminated in 'the Troubles', a series of violent conflicts which began around the late 1960s and is generally agreed to have ended with the Belfast Good Friday' Agreement of 1998.

§2. Amending the Constitution

27. The Constitution is regarded as formal and rigid due to the method of amending the document. Amendment of the Constitution can only take place by popular referendum. According to Article 46, every proposal to amend the Constitution must be initiated in the *Dáil* (lower House) as a Bill. It must then be passed by both Houses of the *Oireachtas* (Parliament) before being submitted to the people. The Bill must be expressly for the purpose of amending the Constitution and it cannot contain any other proposal. If the proposal is approved by a majority of the votes cast at the referendum, the President will sign it into law. Article 46 also specifies that the Constitution may be amended by way of 'variation, addition, or repeal'. However, there is no further guidance in the Constitution as to whether there are any specific limits on the power of the people to amend the Constitution.

28. For a time, there was a question over whether the people could amend the Constitution if the amendment was contrary to the Natural Law. This was because the Constitution had been interpreted as incorporating Natural Law in many judgments in which it seemed to be suggested that Natural Law was antecedent and superior to the Constitution.[32] However, this issue came directly before the courts in the case of *Re Article 26 and the Regulation of Information (Termination of Pregnancies) Bill 1995*.[33] The Bill in question was pursuant to the Fourteenth Amendment, which expressly allowed the *Oireachtas* to legalize the distribution of information on abortion in the State. Before signing the Bill into law, the President exercised her power under Article 26 to send it to the Supreme Court for a decision on its constitutionality.[34] The argument was made that the people's power of amendment did not extend to violating the fundamental principles of Natural Law. However, the Supreme Court disagreed and held that the Constitution is the fundamental and supreme law of the State and that popular sovereignty is the foundation of Irish constitutional law. Therefore, Natural Law could not limit the power of the people to amend the Constitution.

29. Bunreacht na hÉireann has been amended twenty-nine times. Eleven proposed amendments were defeated in referendums. Many of the amendments have been necessitated by changes to the European Union.[35] Of the others, the most notable amendments were those which brought in divorce, marriage equality and the controversial Eighth Amendment on the right to life of the unborn.[36]

I. Difficulties

30. While in theory, the people hold the ultimate power under the Constitution, the reality is somewhat different and in terms of constitutional amendment, the people are completely dependent on the Government to propose a measure to amend the

32. *See McGee v. Attorney General* [1974] IR 284; *G. v. An Bord Uchtala* [1980] IR 32; *Norris v. Attorney General* [1984] IR 36.
33. [1995] 1 IR 1.
34. *See* more at paras 82–85.
35. *See* para. 188.
36. *See* more at paras 218–230.

Constitution. While the earlier 1922 Constitution contained provisions which allowed the people to initiate a referendum[37]under the current Constitution, the people do not have this power and are only involved once the proposal is put before them in a referendum. If constitutional change is desired by the people, their only option is to lobby the Government for change. However, if the issue is one which is seen as politically sensitive, it is not likely to be put before the people due to the fear of losing support in the next election if the referendum is not successful. The exception to this general rule is perhaps the referendum of May 2015, which changed the definition of marriage in the Constitution to allow same-sex couples to marry.

31. Another difficulty which has emerged in relation to amending the Constitution is the issue of funding. In 1995, the Supreme Court held in the case of *McKenna v. An Taoiseach*, that it was unconstitutional for the Government to spend public funds to support one side only of a referendum campaign.[38] The context was a referendum to remove the ban on divorce and it was argued that using public funds to finance only one side violated the equality provision in Article 40.1. To resolve the difficulties raised by this decision, the Referendum Commission was established. This is an independent statutory body which is newly reconstituted in advance of each referendum in order to distribute neutral information on the proposed amendment. The chairperson is usually a retired superior court judge.

32. The result in the *McKenna* case led, perhaps inevitably, to a challenge from the leader of the side which lost the referendum. Des Hanafin argued that the result of the referendum was now uncertain given that funds had been spent unconstitutionally to promote a yes vote. However, it was held that since the vote had been carried out by secret ballot, it would be impossible to prove that the unconstitutional spend of public funds influenced the vote either way. Therefore, the Court felt that it could not upset a democratic vote of the people as expressed in a referendum.[39]

33. The establishment of the Referendum Commission did not put an end to the difficulties surrounding referendums. In 2003, a case arose out of the fact that Raidió Teilifís Éireann (RTE), the national broadcaster, had unfairly allocated political broadcasts during the Divorce campaign, so that, the Yes side received more than four times the airtime the No side received.[40] Their explanation was that RTE was using the same formula as for the distribution of party political broadcasting time among parties at a general election and that they also bore in mind that all the major political parties were on the Yes side. However, the High Court applied the ruling in the 1995 *McKenna* judgment and held that (given that public funds were involved) equality must be given to both sides.

34. More recent controversy surrounded the Children's Rights Referendum in 2012, which added a section on the rights of the Child to the Constitution. Despite the fact that the Referendum Commission distributed neutral information to the public,

---

37. Article 48 of the 1922 Irish Free State Constitution provided for the setting up of the Initiative – a mechanism whereby the people could propose their own laws and constitutional amendments. However, this provision was subsequently removed from the Constitution in 1928 without ever being activated.
38. *McKenna v. An Taoiseach* (No. 2) [1995] 2IR 10.
39. *Hanafin* (n. 17).
40. *Coughlan v. Broadcasting Complaints Commission* [2003] IR 1.

the Government decided to launch its own information campaign in advance of the vote. However, a challenge was brought in relation to the leaflet published by the Government and it was argued that the Government publication was biased in favour of a Yes vote. The Supreme Court held that the Government had acted wrongfully in spending public money on advertising which was not fair and impartial.[41] On foot of this ruling, a subsequent case then challenged the resulting Yes vote but this was again dismissed by the Supreme Court.[42] Similar challenges were also brought against the result of the referendum in 2015 which amended the definition of marriage in the Constitution to include same-sex marriage. However, these attempts were also easily dismissed as being wholly without merit.

35. There is nothing in the Constitution to prevent a failed proposal being resubmitted to the people at a later time. Indeed this is exactly what has happened on a few previous occasions, notably with the Nice and Lisbon Treaty referendums, where in both instances the proposals were successful the second time around. However, there are also examples of proposals which were defeated again on the second attempt, such as the proposal to remove proportional representation as the voting system for elections and the attempts to exclude suicide as grounds for an abortion.

§3. Hierarchy

36. The Constitution is regarded as the highest legal source within Ireland. It takes precedence over all legislation, Common Law and customary law. However, in the case of conflict between an aspect of EU law and the Irish Constitution, the law of the EU takes precedence.

41. *McCrystal v. Minister for Children and Youth Affairs & Ors* [2012] IESC 53.
42. *Jordan v. Minister for Children and Youth Affairs & Ors* [2015] IESC 33. The result in this case was not surprising because the case mirrored the facts in *Hanafin* (n. 17).

Chapter 3. Legislation

37. Legislation, also known as statute law, is the second primary source of law in Ireland, under the Constitution. It consists of laws enacted by the *Oireachtas* (Parliament) and signed into law by the President. These laws are subordinate to the Constitution and in case of conflict with the Constitution; the offending legislative provision will be struck down by the Courts. Thus, legislation has little scope as a source of constitutional law but legislation can be used to provide greater detail and to create a structure around constitutional provisions.

38. Legislation can be categorized as either primary or secondary. Primary legislation comprises Acts of the *Oireachtas* enacted in the manner set out by the Constitution.[43] These are generally further broken down into three categories: Acts to amend the Constitution, public general Acts (for the public at large), and private Acts (for specific groups or authorities). Secondary legislation, also known as subordinate or delegated legislation, normally comprises regulations which provide the detail surrounding general principles already contained in primary legislation. The rules in relation to delegated legislation are considered in Part II.[44]

43. *See* para. 106.
44. *See* paras 111–115.

Chapter 4. Case law

39. Since Ireland is a Common Law system, case law is very important as a source of law. While case law ranks under legislation in the hierarchy of sources, the judgments of the High and Supreme Courts have made a significant contribution to the development of Irish constitutional law, particularly in the area of fundamental rights.

§1. Contribution of Judicial Decisions to Irish Constitutional Law

40. The most significant contribution of judicial decisions to Irish Constitutional Law is the doctrine of unenumerated rights, located in Article 40.3 of the Constitution. This Article provides that 'The State guarantees in its laws to respect, and as far as practicable, by its laws to defend and vindicate the personal rights of the citizen.' It also specifies that 'The State shall, in particular, by its laws protect as best it may from unjust attack and, in the case of injustice done, vindicate the life, person, good name and property rights of every citizen.' Before 1963, it was not considered that any additional rights, beyond those already listed in the subsequent Articles, were conferred by this provision. However, a case brought that year resulted in a complete transformation of the view of this provision and of the constitutional landscape in general. In *Ryan v. Attorney General,*[45] the issue was the constitutionality of the decision to introduce fluoride into the water supply as a health measure.[46] In particular, it was argued that this measure violated the plaintiff's constitutional rights, including her right to bodily integrity. This was not a right mentioned in the Constitution, but it was argued that this right was implicit in Article 40.3. While the plaintiff ultimately lost the case, the High Court and subsequently the Supreme Court, accepted the idea that Article 40.3 contains a guarantee to protect a 'catalogue of unspecified rights in addition to those expressly referred to in the constitutional text'.[47]

41. The courts subsequently went on to 'discover' a ream of further unenumerated rights under this Article. They include the rights not to be tortured or ill-treated,[48] to travel within or outside the State,[49] to communicate[50], to marry,[51] to marital privacy,[52] to individual privacy,[53] to procreate,[54] the rights of an unmarried mother,[55] the rights

45. [1965] IR 294.
46. [1965] IR 294.
47. Raymond Byrne and Paul McCutcheon, *The Irish Legal System* (4th edn, Butterworths, 2001) 552.
48. *The State (C) v. Frawley* [1976] IR 365.
49. *Ryan* (n. 45); *The State (M) v. Attorney General* [1979] IR 73.
50. *Attorney General v. Paperlink* [1984] ILRM 343.
51. *Ryan* (n. 45).
52. *McGee* (n. 32).
53. *Kennedy v. Ireland* [1987] IR 587.
54. *Murray v. Ireland* [1985] IR 532; [1991] ILRM 465.
55. *G v. An Bord Uchtála* [1980] IR 32.

of a child,[56] the right to independent domicile and maintenance[57], to access to the courts,[58] to legal representation,[59] to fair procedures[60] and to earn a livelihood.[61] This catalogue of rights is now generally known as the doctrine of unenumerated rights.

42. The most convincing reason put forward for the emergence of the doctrine in the first place has been described as '*faute de mieux*'.[62] Due to a gap in the Constitution and the reluctance of the legislature to act, the judiciary stepped into the breach. However, recently it has been argued that while the doctrine has been beneficial, it would have been better to have interpreted those rights under existing constitutional provisions rather than the vague notions under which the doctrine was located in Article 40.3.[63] Whether or not this is the correct view, it seems that, for now at least, any further development of the doctrine has stalled. More recently, the Courts have been reluctant to introduce any new unenumerated rights and the trend has involved a renewed focus on the actual text of the Constitution.[64]

43. The development of constitutional jurisprudence is not limited to the field of constitutional rights and many other major legal principles have developed from case law. Here are just a few examples: the case of *Crotty v. An Taoiseach* developed the rules around Ireland's relationship with the EU and the need for referendums,[65] *East Donegal Co-op Ltd. v. the Attorney General* developed the presumption of constitutionality,[66] *Byrne v. Ireland* declared that the State had not inherited the Royal Prerogative and thus has no sovereign immunity from suit,[67] *Murphy v. Attorney General* developed the rules surrounding the retrospective effect of laws which were found to be unconstitutional,[68] *Maguire v. Ardagh* set the constitutional limits on the powers of parliamentary committees.[69]

44. Thus, while the Constitution remains the primary source of law within the State, judicial decisions which interpret and expand on the principles contained within the document are an essential part of the constitutional landscape in Ireland.

---

56. *Re the Adoption (No 2) Bill 1987* [1989] IR 656.
57. *CM v. TM (No 2)* [1991] ILRM 268.
58. *Macauley v. Minister for Posts and Telegraphs* [1966] IR 345.
59. *The State (Healy) v. O'Donoghue* [1976] IR 325.
60. *Re Haughey* [1971] IR 217.
61. *Murphy v. Stewart* [1973] IR 97.
62. *See* Morgan, *Constitutional Law of Ireland* (n. 15) 20.
63. *See* Gerard Hogan, 'The Distorting Effect of Ryan v AG and the Unenumerated Rights Doctrine' in Laura Cahillane, James Gallen and Tom Hickey (eds) *Judges, Politics and the Irish Constitution* (MUP 2016).
64. *See for example TD. v. Minister for Education* [2001] 4 I.R. 259. For more on unenumerated rights *see* paras 196 et seq.
65. [1987] IR 713.
66. [1970] IR 317.
67. [1972] IR 241.
68. [1982] IR 241.
69. [2002] 1 IR 385.

Chapter 5. Customary Law, Unwritten Principles

45. The sole reference to customary law in the Irish Constitution is to customary international law. Article 29.3 states that 'Ireland accepts the generally recognized principles of International Law as its rule of conduct in its relations with other States.' The meaning of this provision came up for consideration in the case of *State (Sumers Jennings) v. Furlong.*[70] The argument made in the case, which related to extradition, was that as a consequence of Article 29.3, all International Law is brought into the Irish Constitution and enjoys the same force as the rest of the Constitution, therefore any law which conflicts with it is invalid. However, the Supreme Court disagreed with this reading of the Article, explaining that it was merely aspirational in character and was simply intended to mean that Ireland would observe the rules of customary International Law in its dealings with other States. This reading of the provision is strengthened if one considers the Irish version of the text. As noted above, Irish language is the first official language under Article 8.1. This means that in the case of a difference between the English and Irish versions of the Constitution, the Irish version would prevail. In the present case, there was no divergence but the Court looked to the Irish version, which uses the words '*ina dtreoir*', which means 'as guidance', as opposed to the English equivalent, 'as its rule of conduct'. The Irish formulation makes the point, even more strongly than the English version, that International Law is not law upon which an individual may rely in an Irish Court; but serves as guidance to the State, in its relations with other States.

46. Customary law in general is regarded as a secondary source of law; it does not enjoy the force of law but may be of use with regard to interpretation of laws. One such example is Canon law.

47. Conventions are a type of unwritten law. Unlike in Britain, where unwritten rules and conventions are of great import, in Ireland most conventions have been adopted in written form, either in the Constitution or in legislation. However, it has been argued that some residual unwritten conventions exist in the Irish system.[71] Examples include the convention that the chairperson of the *Dáil*'s Public Accounts Committee and half of its membership must be members of Opposition parties, the convention that the President should not be publicly criticized by the Government, and the convention of individual ministerial responsibility. However, these would be subordinate to any piece of legislation or constitutional provision and indeed are probably not legally enforceable.

70. [1966] IR 183.
71. *See* Morgan, *Constitutional Law of Ireland* (n. 15) 12.

Chapter 6. Subordinate Rules and Regulations

48. Subordinate or delegated legislation is a secondary form of legislation. It is only legally valid provided certain criteria are complied with. The details are discussed in Part II. All of these subordinate rules, regulations and bye-laws derive their validity from the Constitution.

Chapter 7. Constitutional Interpretation

49. As we shall see below, the Irish Constitution accords considerable power to the higher courts in relation to judicial review and interpretation of the Constitution. Despite this however, the Constitution provides little guidance as to how this power ought to be exercised. While limited guidance can be found for certain sections, such as those dealing with the structure of the courts and the institutions of government, many other areas such as the fundamental rights provisions are quite vague. As a result of this and due to the need for consistency and clarity, the Irish Courts have devised various methods of constitutional interpretation. They differ somewhat from the methods of statutory interpretation, which have been deemed unsuitable for constitutional purposes and while various different interpretive methods have been in vogue at different times, the contemporary uses and contexts of the various methods are set out below.

§1. The Literal Approach

50. There are some provisions, usually technical in nature rather than rights provisions, for which the courts have decided a literal interpretation is most suitable. In the case of *The People (DPP) v. O'Shea*, O'Higgins CJ made the following helpful comment on the use of the approach:

> The Constitution, as the fundamental law of the State, must be accepted, interpreted and construed according to the words which are used; and those words, where the meaning is plain and unambiguous, must be given their literal meaning. Of course, the Constitution must be looked at as a whole and not merely in parts and, where doubt or ambiguity exists, regard may be had to other provisions of the Constitution and to the situation which obtained and the laws which were in force when it was enacted. Plain words must, however, be given their plain meaning unless qualified or restricted by the Constitution itself.[72]

There are advantages and disadvantages to this approach. First, it allows the courts to follow the actual language of the text of the Constitution, something which guards against a wide scope for judicial interpretation. Disadvantages include the fact that courts may sometimes have to fall back on standard Common Law principles of statutory interpretation which have been declared as unsuitable for this task. Furthermore, a meaning which is plain to one judge may not be so to another and problems of construction may arise. This approach was the principal approach taken for many years. During the 1970s, there seemed to be some judicial unease with the strict nature of this approach which precipitated various other methods coming to the fore. However, recent years have largely seen a return to the literal approach, with many judges following the advice of O'Higgins to look to the text of the Constitution and then, if

72. [1982] IR 384, 397.

there is any doubt as to its meaning, consider adopting one of the other interpretive approaches to settle the apparent ambiguity.

§2. The Historical Approach

51. It can sometimes be helpful to the court, in interpreting the Constitution, to have regard to the history of the Constitution or the state of affairs and public opinion at the time of its enactment. However, historical considerations are not always helpful or suitable and can sometimes even lead to confusion, as in the *Sinnott Case,*[73] where it was held that the words 'primary education' must be interpreted by reference to the practice in 1937 even though it was also held that the word 'child' must be given its modern meaning (i.e. under the age of 18). While this approach has been used from time to time, it is not generally resorted to and in particular, it has been recognized that it is not an appropriate method when interpreting fundamental rights provisions. As such, it is of limited practical benefit. However, it may still be useful, particularly when combined with a purposive approach. Indeed, Professor Kelly has suggested that where the Constitution carefully defines certain powers, rights, privileges and procedures, the courts must carefully follow the text of the Constitution, aided, where necessary, by a historical understanding of the framers' intention.[74] However, because the fundamental rights provisions were left deliberately vague and ambiguous, it would seem that these were expected to change with social values.

§3. The Natural Law Approach

52. At times, the Courts have used extra-constitutional principles in interpreting the text of the Constitution, sometimes referencing 'higher law' or 'natural law'. However, the approach has not been consistent and while in the past, this approach was in vogue with many judges and indeed played a pivotal role in the development of the fundamental rights provisions in the Constitution, today it has fallen out of favour, possibly as a result of a realization that this approach is not reliable as the standards and opinions involved are necessarily subjective. It is doubtful that this approach will have anything but a limited application in future and will most likely be used solely as a last resort by the judiciary to resolve 'hard cases' in such a way as to avoid a patent injustice.

§4. The Broad/Purposive/Harmonious Approach

53. The objective of the broad, or purposive approach, is to allow judges to be guided by the actual language of the Constitution but to avoid the excessive formalism of the literal approach. This approach involves an attempt to identify the main purpose and objective of the provision and so judges need not have recourse to the standard

73. *Sinnott v. Minister for Education* [2001] 2 I.R. 545.
74. Hogan and Whyte, *J M Kelly: The Irish Constitution* (n. 9) 24.

Common Law methods of interpretation. This approach has been used in a number of cases, particularly where the literal approach has not been helpful.

54. The Harmonious approach can be regarded as a variation of the broad approach. The idea is that the Constitution should be construed as a whole and that provisions should not be considered in isolation. It has been described as 'no more than a presumption that the people who enacted the Constitution had a single scale of values, and wished those values to permeate their charter evenly and without internal discordance'.[75] Such an approach has proved useful in a number of cases and has also been used to reconcile competing constitutional rights. However, as with the natural law approach, the doctrine of harmonious interpretation can also allow the courts to override the text of the Constitution in preference for extra-constitutional principles, which can be highly subjective. Thus, unless this approach remains grounded in the text of the Constitution, it too can be problematic.

55. Furthermore, this approach does not take into account the fact that certain constitutional provisions may be at odds with each other. Doyle gives the example of the relationship of freedom of religious conscience in Article 44.2.1 and the prohibition on religious discrimination in Article 44.2.3°. In the case of *Quinn's Supermarket v. Attorney General*,[76] the Court recognized that there could be a potential conflict between the two provisions and in order to resolve this it looked at the overall purpose of Article 44 and interpreted the prohibition in Article 44.2.3° to be subordinate to what was perceived as the stronger guarantee of free practice. But as Doyle points out, it is 'arguable that the purpose of a guarantee against religious discrimination is to prohibit religious discrimination, not to facilitate the free practice of religion' and by interpreting the prohibition as 'subordinate to the guarantee of free practice, the courts have – in the interests of harmony – turned Article 44.2.3° into a virtual dead-letter.'[77] Doyle argues that a better approach would be to give due weight to both competing provisions. Although he acknowledges that it might, in certain particular instances, be difficult to work out which provision should be given greater weight on balance.

§5. A Balanced Approach

56. There is no one perfect rule for constitutional interpretation and each of the different approaches has their own advantages and disadvantages. It is generally a question of balance and knowing which approach to use in which particular case. Professor Kelly has suggested a useful approach which balances the historical approach with a 'present tense' approach. He has written that the 'present tense' approach is appropriate for standards and values. So elements, such as personal rights, the 'common good', social justice, equality etc. should be interpreted 'according to the lights of today as the judges perceive and share them.' He felt that the historical approach is appropriate where 'some law-based system is in issue, like jury trial, county councils, the census'. He notes that these were 'built into the case of the state' and if their removal or transformation is needed 'it must be authorized by the people in a referendum; they

---

75. *Ibid* 8.

76. [1972] IR 1.

77. Oran Doyle, *Constitutional Law: Text, Cases and Materials* (Clarus Press, 2008) 459-60.

cannot be whittled away by ordinary legislation subject only to "present tense" constitutional scrutiny.' However, he also notes that this does not mean that such systems are 'fixed in the permafrost of 1937':

> The courts ought to have some leeway for considering which dimensions of a system are secondary, and which are so material to traditional constitutional values that a willingness to see them diluted or substantially abolished without a referendum could not be imputed to the enacting electorate.[78]

While this so-called standards/technicalities distinction can also be difficult to apply in certain cases, it at least offers some logical guidance.

§6. Further Constitutional Principles

I. Hierarchy of Rights

57. As a result of the doctrine of harmonious interpretation mentioned above, questions arose as to whether there exists a hierarchy of rights within the Constitution. There was some recognition of this possibility in early cases where a conflict of provisions emerged[79] but a clear acknowledgment of a hierarchy was made by the Supreme Court in the case of *The People v. Shaw*.[80] This case centred on the lawfulness of the continued detention of a murder suspect by *Gardaí* who had hoped to use the suspect to help them find the victim alive. In allowing evidence obtained during the potentially illegal detention, the Court recognized that a hierarchy of constitutional values exists and that when a conflict arises, the right which ranks higher must prevail. Here it was concluded that the suspect's right to personal liberty was outweighed by the need to rescue a victim in peril.

58. While the existence of this hierarchy has been referred to in numerous subsequent cases, there is no clear guidance available as to how to determine which right is to be given precedence and it appears that this is decided by the judiciary on a case-by-case basis. It is also clear from the case law that the hierarchy is to be applied only in exceptional circumstances as an injustice could easily result from its abuse.

II. Presumption of Constitutionality

59. The presumption of constitutionality was first recognized by O'Dalaigh CJ in *Ryan v. Attorney General*[81] He explained that: 'There is a presumption that a statute

78. Hogan and Whyte, *JM Kelly: The Irish Constitution*, (n. 9) 24, Kelly, 'Law and Manifesto' in Litton (ed.), *The Constitution of Ireland 1937-1987* (n. 30).
79. *The Quinn's case* [1972] IR 1; *McMahon v. Attorney General* [1972] IR 69; *Dillon-Leetch v. Calleary* (no. 1) (31 Jul. 1974 SC).
80. [1982] IR 1.
81. *Ryan* (n. 45).

is constitutional and the onus of showing that it is unconstitutional rests on the plaintiff who attacks it.' It works in a similar way to the presumption of innocence in criminal law. There are two aspects to this idea – first, relating to the onus of proof in constitutional cases and also to the interpretation of challenged statutes. However, in relation to the second aspect, where the challenged legislation is clearly in violation of a constitutional provision, the presumption will not apply. The presumption also applies to bills that have been referred to the Supreme Court under Article 26.[82] In such instances the bill is presumed to be constitutional and legal counsel is appointed by the Court to argue the case for unconstitutionality.

60. Related to the presumption, is the double construction rule, which mandates that if a piece of legislation is vague, to the extent that one reading of it would lead to an unconstitutionality whereas another reading would mean the legislation was consistent with the Constitution, then the interpretation which is consistent with the Constitution must prevail. This rule was enunciated in the case of *East Donegal Co-op Ltd. v. Attorney Gen.*[83] This rule can cut down on the scope of the provision or may force the court to take a narrow interpretation of the challenged provision.

61. There are limits to the rule however, as was pointed out in the *East Donegal* case; if the words are clear and the statute is still invalid then it cannot be interpreted in any other manner. As Casey has put it: 'The constitutional construction which the courts are obliged to prefer must be one that is fairly and reasonably open given the language used. It is not open for the courts to indulge in legislating, under the guise of interpreting.'[84]

62. Another related practice is the idea that if a case can be decided on non-constitutional grounds it will be done accordingly. Constitutional issues will only be considered by the superior courts in the absence of any other deciding factors. This idea comes from the American constitutional notion of 'mootness'. It was first accepted by the Irish Supreme Court in the case of *Condon v. Minister for Labour*.[85]

---

82. *See* paras 82–85.
83. [1970] IR 317.
84. James Casey, *Constitutional Law in Ireland* (3rd edn, Round Hall, 2000) 367.
85. [1981] IR 62.

Part II. Form of Government

Chapter 1. General

§1. Introduction

63. In Article 5 of Bunreacht na hÉireann, Ireland is described as a sovereign, independent, democratic State. Although Ireland is often described as a republic, and the name 'Republic of Ireland' is often used to distinguish the State from Northern Ireland, which is part of the United Kingdom, the word republic is not found in the Constitution. There are historic reasons for this.

64. As noted above, the 1922 Irish Free State Constitution was the first Constitution of the modern Irish State. As a result of the Anglo-Irish Treaty, agreed between representatives of Great Britain and Ireland in 1921, the new Irish Free State was given dominion status. Throughout the years of the Free State, attempts were made to distance Ireland from Britain and many of the references to the Crown or to other British elements, which had been insisted upon by the British during the drafting stages of the Constitution, were gradually removed from the Constitution. In 1937, when the new Constitution was promulgated, the Irish Free State was still legally in existence and because of the External Relations Act 1936, Ireland was still in the Commonwealth. There are a number of reasons for the avoidance of the word republic at this time; first, Ireland was still partitioned and it may have been felt in some quarters that the declaration of a republic without having achieved a united Ireland would be a betrayal of the Easter Rising of 1916; the use of the word might also have angered Unionists in the North and the South, supporters of dominion status in Ireland, and the British. Also, at the time, declaring a republic would have meant leaving the Commonwealth and it suited Ireland, for economic reasons, to remain within this entity. However, *de facto* independence had already been achieved with the passing by the British Parliament of the Statute of Westminster 1931, which gave autonomy to the Dominions, and in 1945, in response to a question in the *Dáil* about the status of the State, Taoiseach Eamon de Valera replied, with what became known as his 'Dictionary Republic' speech, that Ireland was a republic in everything but name. In fact it was not until 1949 that Ireland officially became a republic with the passing of The Republic of Ireland Act 1948, which provided a legislative basis for the description of the State as a republic. However, the Constitution remains unchanged.

65. The central branches of government in Ireland may be described briefly as consisting of the following:

(1) The legislative branch, which is known as the *Oireachtas* and comprises the President and the two Houses of Parliament; *Dáil Éireann* and *Seanad Éireann.*
(2) The executive branch, which is the Government, consisting of the *Taoiseach* (Prime Minister) and up to fourteen other Ministers. The Government is chosen by the *Dáil* and holds office for the same term (the Constitution sets a maximum term of seven years but a five-year term has been set by legislation), unless it loses a vote of no confidence in the *Dáil*, in which case it must resign.
(3) The judiciary, which is independent of the other branches of government.

66. These branches will be analysed separately below. First, it is necessary to elaborate briefly on the relationship between them. While the Constitution does not specifically impose the idea of the 'Separation of Powers', Article 6, which proclaims that 'All powers of government, legislative, executive and judicial, derive under God, from the people ...', has been interpreted as incorporating the idea. There are dicta from judges in many cases alluding to this including *Re Haughey*,[86] *State (C) v. Minister for Justice*,[87] *Melling v. O Mathghamhna*,[88] and *Crotty v. An Taoiseach*,[89] where Finlay CJ pointed out that that the separation of powers is fundamental to the Constitution.

67. The principle idea behind the separation of powers is to limit government power so as to prevent corruption and autocracy. It involves dividing governmental authority among different bodies, with each one having a degree of independence so as to act as a 'counter-balance' against the others.[90] However, while the separation of powers is clearly an important element in the Irish Constitution, Ireland does not follow the theory strictly and while the judiciary is an independent branch, the other two branches have been described as fused. Members of the Government are also members of the *Oireachtas* and while in theory the Government is responsible to the *Dáil*, in reality, the Government parties usually control the *Oireachtas*. This will become clear below.

§2. Political Structure – Parties

68. In Ireland, there is a multi-party political system. This is mainly due to the electoral system and the use of Proportional Representation with the Single Transferable Vote (PR-STV). Political parties are not explicitly acknowledged in the Constitution.

69. The two biggest parties in Ireland have traditionally been *Fine Gael* and *Fianna Fáil* which both originate from disagreements regarding the Treaty settlement of 1921. *Fine Gael* is the party which developed out of the 'Pro-treaty 'faction , who went into Government with the Labour party following the general election in 1922

86. *Haughey* (n. 60).
87. [1967] IR 1.
88. [1962] IR 1.
89. *Crotty* (n. 16).
90. *See* Morgan, *Constitutional Law of Ireland* (n. 15) 33.

and set about establishing the new Irish State. *Fianna Fáil* developed around its charismatic leader, Eamon de Valera, the only surviving leader of the Easter Rising of 1916, who originally refused to accept the Treaty and refused to take his seat in Parliament. De Valera eventually returned to parliamentary politics with his new party and came to power in 1932. From then until the economic crash of the late 2000s, *Fianna Fáil* was the dominant force in Irish party politics. The 2011 general election saw the greatest ever loss of *Fianna Fáil* seats and led to a coalition between *Fine Gael* and Labour. While originally there were historic differences between both parties, today there is very little to separate them. They are both Centre-right parties with broadly similar policies.

70. Of the other parties, the oldest and until recently, the most successful is the Labour party. It was founded in 1912 as the political wing of the Irish Trade Union Congress. It has been in coalition governments a number of times, mostly with *Fine Gael*. While the Labour party would have been seen historically as the worker's party and would have received much of the Left vote, in recent years other groupings have established themselves more firmly as Leftist organizations. Another party that describes itself as Left-wing is *Sinn Féin*. While this party holds the name of the organization credited with the Easter Rising of 1916 and still maintains that it is a republican party seeking to end British rule in Northern Ireland, it has little in common with the original *Sinn Féin*, many members of which went on to become members of the two larger parties. The modern *Sinn Féin* party can be traced back to 1970, when a dispute over abstentionism led to a split, the anti-abstentionists forming the Worker's party and the others maintaining the name *Sinn Féin*, became the political wing of the Irish Republican Army (IRA), an extreme paramilitary organization. Today, *Sinn Féin* has distanced itself from its IRA links and has become a more mainstream, Left-wing party.

71. Presently, there are a few small parties in the *Dáil*, such as the Anti-Austerity Alliance – People Before Profit Party, the Green Party and the Social Democrats as well as some other independent groupings. In the past, various other smaller parties emerged, though many of them did not last long. They can be categorized as follows: The Farmers' Party, the National Centre Party and *Clann na Talmhan* were agrarian; *Clann Éireann*, *Aontacht Éireann* and *Clann na Poblachta* were Republican; there were many left-wing groups – the National Progressive Democrats, the Workers' Party, the Socialist Labour Party, the Democratic Socialist Party and the National Labour Party. The National League was a party which favoured remaining within the British Commonwealth and maintaining close ties with Britain in the 1920s and *Ailtirí na hAiséighe* was a radical nationalist and fascist party in the 1940s and 1950s. The Progressive Democrats, not to be confused with a party of a similar name above, was a more successful, conservative-liberal party which existed from 1985 to 2009. It participated in a number of coalition governments but many people blamed the recent financial and economic crisis on Progressive Democrat policies and so the Party did not survive the downturn.

72. Recent years have also seen the rise of Independent politicians. While Independents have always been part of the political scene in Ireland, disfavour with many of the political parties in recent years has led to an unprecedented number of Independents in the current *Dáil*, which in turn led to months of uncertainty following the last general election, since no party could form a majority government. Because

Independents are not affiliated with any particular party they usually stand on local interests and many are primarily interested in developments in their own constituencies rather than with national affairs. The current administration will be a fascinating study for posterity as it relies on the support of at least six Independents to remain in power.

§3. Referendum and Popular Initiative

73. The referendum is an important part of the Irish Constitution. According to Article 47, amendment of the Constitution is by referendum only. The provision states that a proposal to amend the Constitution shall have been approved by the people if a majority of the votes cast at the referendum shall have been cast in favour of its enactment into law. While the present Constitution has been in force for less than eighty years, there have been over thirty referendums, some of them involving multiple issues. In more recent times, many of the referendums have been due to changes in the European Union. Ireland voted to accede to the European Communities in 1973 and an amendment was inserted into the Constitution to allow for this. However any major change to this Community, not originally envisaged in 1973 requires a new amendment to the Constitution and therefore another referendum.

74. Under the 1922 Irish Free State Constitution, there was also the possibility of a legislative referendum and popular initiative under Articles 47 and 48. The legislative referendum would have operated as a sort of veto whereby if the people were unhappy with a piece of legislation about to be passed, they could petition the *Oireachtas* to hold a referendum to decide the issue. First, the Bill could be suspended on the written demand of two-fifths of the members of the *Dáil* or of a majority of the members of the *Seanad* and then a petition signed by no less than one-twentieth of the registered voters could instigate the referendum. The initiative would have worked in a similar way. Proposals could have been initiated by the petition of fifty thousand registered voters and if rejected by the *Oireachtas*, the measure would have been put to a referendum. However, neither of these two provisions was ever activated. When an attempt was made to bring a petition to remove the oath of faithfulness to the King from the Constitution in 1928, the Government of the day simply decided to pre-empt this move and promptly removed both provisions from the Constitution.[91]

75. While there is no equivalent in the Constitution today, there is a more limited procedure still available under Article 27. Under this provision, a majority of the *Seanad* and at least a third of the *Dáil* can petition the President not to sign a bill into law and instead to ascertain the will of the people. This procedure can only be initiated under the conditions set down in Article 23, where the *Seanad* has rejected a bill passed by the *Dáil* or has passed it with amendments which are unacceptable to the *Dáil* and

91. While the oath was a controversial and unwelcome inclusion it was something which was insisted upon by the British. The Government removed Articles 47 and 48 from the Constitution, not because they disagreed with the notion of popular sovereignty but because they feared for the consequences if the Opposition had succeeded with the proposal to remove the oath.

the *Dáil* passes a resolution which deems the bill to have been passed.[92] However this procedure has never been attempted.

92. Since the *Dáil* is traditionally the more powerful House, it can effectively bypass the *Seanad* in the legislative process; while the *Seanad* can delay legislation, it cannot block it.

Chapter 2. Head of State

§1. The Organ of State

76. The Head of State in Ireland is the President. The earlier 1922 Constitution did not provide for a President. Because of the restraints on the drafters due to the Treaty settlement, it was provided for in that document that the British Crown, represented by the Governor-General would constitute the Head of State. The office of the President was established under the current 1937 Constitution and was not without controversy. Due to international developments at the time, Opposition Parties wished for confirmation that the role would not evolve into a dictatorship. Because of these concerns, most of the powers conferred on the President are purely ceremonial; many of the decisions involved are taken 'on the advice of the Government' which means that it is actually the Government who decides.

77. Articles 12 and 13 provide detail on the role of the President. While the Constitution does not actually use the term 'Head of State', this omission is clarified by Article 12.1, which states that the President takes precedence over all other persons in the State. Taking this into consideration along with the other various ceremonial functions assigned to the President, it is clear that the President is, in fact, the Head of State.

78. According to Article 15.2.2°, the President is part of the *Oireachtas* and therefore technically is part of the legislature. However, the President does not have the power to determine the content of laws and must sign every bill put before him, unless the procedures in Articles 26 or 27 are invoked.[93]

79. The President is elected directly by the people of Ireland and serves a term of seven years.[94] The President may be removed from office on the basis of permanent incapacity or may be impeached. Article 12.10.1° sets out the impeachment procedure in detail. It is based on a similar provision in the Constitution of the United States.

§2. Competence: Powers and Duties

80. As mentioned above, most of the powers of the President are purely formal and are exercised on the advice of the Government or the *Taoiseach*. These are often referred to as the powers or duties of the President in his role as Head of State. Such powers include summoning and dissolving the *Dáil*, signing bills into law, appointing Ministers and other office holders, and acting as Supreme Commander of the Defence

93. *See* paras 82 et seq.
94. Article 12.2.1°.

Forces.[95] The Constitution does allow for further powers to be conferred on the President by statute but these would be subject to the same conditions, i.e. they would be exercised only on the advice of the Government. However, the President also has another important role as 'Guardian of the Constitution' and exercises some more power in this role.

I. Powers and Duties as Guardian of the Constitution

81. When exercising these functions as Guardian of the Constitution, the President acts on his own discretion. However, these powers are quite limited and many have never been exercised. The most significant power vested in the President is the procedure under Article 26 which allows the President to refer a bill to the Supreme Court for consideration as to its constitutionality.

A. Referring a Bill to the Supreme Court for a Decision as to Its Constitutionality

82. Article 26 gives power to the President to refer a Bill to the Supreme Court for a decision on its validity, if there is any doubt as to its constitutionality. As with many of the President's powers, before making a decision, he is obliged to consult the Council of State[96] but the final decision lies with the President. While many Presidents have a firm background in Constitutional law and have not had any difficulty in deciding when to refer cases to the Supreme Court, apart from the Council of State, there is no guidance available to a President who may not have the requisite legal knowledge and there is no possibility of obtaining independent legal advice.

83. This power may be used for most Bills except Money Bills, Constitution Amendment Bills or Bills passed under Article 24. There are also very strict time limits imposed: the reference must be made no later than seven days after the Bill has been presented to the President for his signature, so the President has just one week in which to consult the Council of State and decide whether or not to refer the Bill. If the Supreme Court decides that the Bill, or any part of it, is in fact unconstitutional, the President must refuse to sign it. If however, it is decided that the Bill is valid then it must be signed by the President 'as soon as may be' following the decision.

84. This procedure has proved useful in many ways: it allows for a declaration of unconstitutionality before legislation has been passed, thus avoiding any possible breaches afterwards; it gives certainty to the law if the Supreme has decided that the bill is consistent with the Constitution; it allows the Supreme Court to consider the perspective of those who might not otherwise be able to bring a constitutional challenge to an allegedly unconstitutional provision (take for example the case of the unborn

95. Article 13.6 also bestows on the President the right to commute or remit any punishment imposed by a Court but specifies that this power 'may also be conferred by law on other authorities'. This power is currently exercised by the Minister for Justice by virtue of s. 23(3) of The Criminal Justice Act 1951, as substituted by s. 17 of The Criminal Justice (Miscellaneous Provisions) Act 1997.

96. *See* paras 92–93.

child); and it also allows the Supreme Court to consider the potential unconstitutionality of legislation without having to also look at a particular factual scenario.

85. Despite its utility, there are also a number of disadvantages with the procedure. One major issue is that once the Supreme Court has decided that the bill under reference is consistent with the Constitution, that law then becomes impervious and can never again be questioned by the Courts, even in the case of new factual data or scenarios arising which had not originally been anticipated. This has been referred to as the 'seal of constitutionality' and it can influence the President's decision on whether or not to refer the bill. Also, because there are no real parties involved, the Court must make its decision in a vacuum and therefore it has to imagine hypothetical scenarios but those involved may fail to envisage potential future implications of the bill. Other difficulties include: the fact that the period of time during which the Supreme Court can consider the bill is quite short, particularly when the legislation in question might be lengthy and complicated, the fact that only the President can make the reference to the Supreme Court and he cannot be forced to do so. Furthermore, even if only one provision in a piece of legislation is found to be unconstitutional, the whole bill fails, even if the remainder is unproblematic.

B. Referring a Bill to the People for a Referendum

86. A similar, if more complicated procedure exists under Article 27, which allows for a very limited possibility of forcing a referendum over a bill being debated in the *Oireachtas*. In order for this to happen, a bill passed by the *Dáil* would have to be rejected by the *Seanad* or passed subject to amendments which are unacceptable to the *Dáil*. Then under Article 27, if a majority of Senators and no less than a third of Deputies petition the President not to sign the bill, the President may decline to do so. The President must consider the petition, consult the Council of State and make a decision within six days. During this time, the main question for the consideration of the President is whether the Bill contains a proposal of such national importance that the will of the people ought to be ascertained. If the President believes that the people ought to be consulted, he will then inform the *Taoiseach,* as well as the chairpersons of both Houses that he will not sign the bill unless it is approved in a referendum.[97] If the bill is subsequently approved by the people, then the President must sign it. However, this procedure has never been employed.

C. Dissolving the Dáil under Article 13.2.2°

87. Another potentially significant power exists under Article 13.2.2°. Normally the *Dáil* is summoned and dissolved by the President on the advice of the *Taoiseach* under Article 13.2.1°. However, if the *Taoiseach* loses the support of a majority in the *Dáil,* Article 13.2.2 provides that the President, in his absolute discretion, may refuse to dissolve the *Dáil*. There are a number of reasons for this; for example, if a stable government could be formed from existing representation or if it would not be in the interests of the country to have a general election. The President is not obliged to state his reasons for refusal and the decision cannot be questioned because of Article 13.8.1°,

97. Or until such time as it is approved by a resolution of the new *Dáil* following a general election.

which provides that the President shall not be answerable to either House of the *Oireachtas* or to any court for the exercise and performance of any powers of the office.[98]

88. To date this power has not been expressly invoked by any President in such a circumstance although there have been occasions where the potential power of the provision has been felt. By way of example, in 1994 the then President of Ireland Mary Robinson let it be known through unofficial channels that if the then *Taoiseach* Albert Reynolds was to seek a dissolution of the *Dáil* that she was ready to refuse it due to the fact that an alternative Government could have been formed without an election. It is important to note here that Albert Reynolds had not actually lost a vote in the *Dáil* but his collation partners had made it clear publically that they no longer supported him as *Taoiseach*.[99] Ultimately Albert Reynolds did not push the issue and an alternative Government was formed.

D. Referring a Question on a Money Bill to a Committee of Privileges

89. The significance of this power is that if it a bill is a money bill, then the time during which the *Seanad* may consider it is much shorter than normal. If a dispute arises as to whether a bill is a money bill then the *Seanad* can request the President to refer the issue to a Committee of Privileges (Article 22.2.2°), the President must also consult the Council of State but ultimately, the decision to refer the bill lies with the President. This power has never been exercised.

E. Consenting to Abridge the Time Allowed to the Seanad to Consider a Bill

90. Article 24 allows the Government to curtail the length of time during which the *Seanad* may consider a Bill. This is only if the *Taoiseach* certifies it as 'urgently and immediately necessary'. The *Dáil* may then (by resolution) specify a particular time period for the *Seanad*. Once the period has elapsed, the Bill is deemed to have been passed (Article 24.2). This procedure effectively cuts the *Seanad* out of the legislative process. However, as a safeguard, the President must agree to the resolution that shortens the length of time for the *Seanad*. The Council of State must also be consulted but the President has the final decision on whether to abridge the time allowed to the *Seanad* to consider a bill. The exception is that this procedure cannot be used for bills which propose to amend the Constitution. This power has never been invoked.

---

98. It applies however, only to the exercise of the powers or functions within his/her own discretion. For example, Finlay P commented in *The State (Walshe) v. Murphy* [1981] IR 275 that this does not prevent judicial review of a function which 'require[s] his intervention for its effectiveness in law, [but is] in fact the decision and act of the Executive.'

99. *See also* the Nigerian case of *Adegbenro v. Akintola* [1963] AC 614 which was heard by the Privy Council and concerned a power similar to that in 13.2.2.

F. Addressing the Houses of the Oireachtas and the Nation

91. Under Article 13.2.3°, the President has the power to convene a meeting of the *Oireachtas*, it can be one or both Houses. This power has never been exercised. It may be an emergency provision to allow for calling a meeting of Parliament if there is no alternative means of doing so. In addition, it seems that the extent of the power is simply the convening of the meeting as the President cannot address the parliament without Government approval. The President does have a right of Expression under Articles 13.7.1° and 13.7.2° to address the *Oireachtas* and the Nation respectively. However, the issue must be one of national importance, the Council of State must be consulted and according to subsection 3 the address must first have received the approval of the Government.

§3. Related Bodies

I. The Council of State

92. The Council is an advisory body for the President in the exercise of his/her discretionary powers. As we have seen, Articles 22, 24, 26 and 27 specifically refer to the obligation to consult with the Council. These are then reinforced by Article 32, which states:

> The President shall not exercise or perform any of the powers or functions which are by this constitution expressed to be exercisable or performable by him after consultation with the council of state unless, and on every occasion before so doing, he shall have convened a meeting of the council of state and the members present at such meeting shall have been heard by him.

93. Article 31 lays down the details of the Council. Membership of the Council consists of the *Taoiseach*, the *Tánaiste*, the Chief Justice, the President of the High Court, the *Ceann Comhairle* (chairperson of the *Dáil*), the *Cathaoirleach* (chair) of the Seanad, the Attorney General, any former President, *Taoiseach* or Chief Justice willing and able to act as a member and up to seven other members appointed by the President in his absolute discretion. These members will only serve during that particular Presidential term (as per Article 31.5).[100]

100. Casey describes the inclusion of the Chief Justice and President of the High Court as unusual. Due to the nature of their respective offices these would be useful sources to consult especially concerning Article 26 references. However, as Casey also notes one or both judges may have to sit in the Supreme Court if the Bill is actually referred and this may inhibit them from expressing their views, which significantly negates their usefulness. Kelly has remarked on this point that although prior judicial involvement in a discussion of this kind would be generally regarded as undesirable, this procedure is in fact constitutionally sanctioned. Hogan and Whyte, *JM Kelly: The Irish Constitution* (n. 9) 599.

II. The Presidential Commission

94. Article 14 provides for the assembly of a Presidential Commission to act in place of the President in circumstances where the President is absent, abroad, temporarily or permanently incapacitated or has simply failed to perform the duties of the President. Membership includes the Chief Justice and the chairmen of both Houses of the *Oireachtas*. The Commission has acted a few times, most notably following the death of President Childers in 1974, the resignation of President O'Dálaigh in 1976 and the resignation of President Robinson in 1997. In 1992, when President Robinson was abroad, the Commission granted a dissolution of the *Dáil*.

Chapter 3. Legislature

§1. The Organ of State

95. The Irish legislature is the *Oireachtas*. It is bicameral and, as noted above, according to Article 15.2.2°, the *Oireachtas* also comprises the President. The lower House is referred to as *Dáil Éireann* (the *Dáil*) and the upper House is referred to as *Seanad Éireann* (the *Seanad* or Senate).

96. The original reason for the inclusion of a bicameral legislature in the earlier 1922 Constitution was to provide for representation of the Southern Unionist minority in the *Seanad.* While political difficulties led to the abolition of the *Seanad* in 1936, it was re-established under the current Constitution. However, the question of whether a bicameral legislature is necessary in Ireland has recently arisen again and in 2013, a referendum was held which proposed to abolish the *Seanad.* While the referendum was ultimately defeated, it was clear that there is a desire amongst the people of Ireland for significant reform of the *Seanad.* To date, no such reform has taken place.

I. The Dáil

97. The *Dáil*, because it is the popularly elected House, is by far the more powerful. It currently comprises 157 members, who are referred to as TD's (*Teachtaí Dála*), elected from forty constituencies. All citizens aged 18 years or over may vote in a *Dáil* election. The Ninth Amendment to the Constitution in 1984 also extended this right to British citizens living in Ireland.[101] Voting is by proportional representation. The *Dáil* nominates the *Taoiseach* and approves the other members of Government. The Government is responsible to the *Dáil* and on ceasing to retain a majority there, the *Taoiseach* must resign.

II. The Seanad

98. The *Seanad* has sixty members at present, elected as follows: six members are elected by university graduates – three from the National University of Ireland and

101. Section 8(2) of The Electoral Act 1992 contains the detail on this. It also provides that nationals of other EU Member States are entitled to register to vote provided that the Minister for the Environment is of the opinion that the laws of the other State allow Irish residents to vote in parliament elections for that State and makes an order to that effect. However, no such order has ever been made.

three from the University of Dublin;[102] eleven members are appointed by the *Taoiseach* and forty-three members are elected by local government officials as well as incoming TD's and outgoing Senators. Due to the manner in which Senators are chosen, it is usual for the Government Party to hold a majority in the *Seanad* also.

III. Term, Dissolution and Elections

99. Article 16.5 sets the maximum term of the *Dáil* at seven years but provides that shorter periods may be fixed by law. Section 7 of The Electoral (Amendment) Act 1927 had fixed the *Dáil* term at five years and since it was not repealed, it remained in force under the new Constitution. As a result, the maximum term of the *Dáil* remained five years. This was subsequently confirmed by section 33 of The Electoral Act, 1992.

100. As long as the *Taoiseach* holds a majority in the *Dáil*, he has discretion as to when to call an election within the five-year period. When he wishes to dissolve the *Dáil*, he requests a dissolution from the President who, as noted above, is required to grant the dissolution unless the *Taoiseach* has lost majority support, in which case the President may choose whether or not to grant the dissolution. In order to bring about the dissolution, the President issues a proclamation and a general election must then be held within thirty days. After the President issues the proclamation, the Clerk of the *Dáil* issues a writ to the returning officer in each constituency directing them to hold an election of the prescribed number of members. The Minister for Housing, Planning and Local Government appoints the polling day, which must be within eighteen and twenty-five days (excluding Good Friday, Sundays and public holidays) of the issue of the writ. The Minister must also appoint a polling period which consists of at least twelve hours between 7 a.m. and 10.30 p.m. that day.

101. The Constitution does not mention dissolution of the *Seanad* but Article 18.9 states that: 'Every member of *Seanad Éireann* shall, unless he previously dies, resigns or becomes disqualified, continue to hold office until the day before the polling day of the general election for *Seanad Éireann* next held after his election of nomination.' The fact that the elections for the *Seanad* are not held on one particular polling day, due to the different methods of election, has not yet caused any difficulty.

102. Article 18.8 states that the *Seanad* election, for both university and panel seats, must take place no later than ninety days after the *Dáil* is dissolved. This means that the new *Dáil*, which forms part of the electorate for the *Seanad*, will already be in place before the *Seanad* is elected.

---

102. This system has been described as discriminatory, as graduates from other universities and third level institutions are excluded. While the seventh amendment in 1979 allowed for the extension of the franchise to other similar institutions, this has never been acted upon. There are also now calls to open up the electorate completely as there appears to be no justification for arbitrarily restricting the franchise in this way.

§2. Legal Status

103. Certain privileges attach to the Houses of the *Oireachtas* under Articles 15.10, 15.12 and 15.13. Official reports, publications and all utterances made in either house are privileged. Furthermore, no member of either House can be forced, either in a court of law or in a tribunal, to reveal the source of information used in the course of a parliamentary statement. Members are also immune from arrest and detention, except in certain criminal cases, where they are going to, coming from or within the *Oireachtas*.

104. Article 15.13 guarantees freedom of speech to parliamentarians and in the case of *Attorney General v. Hamilton (no. 2),*[103] the Supreme Court held that this protects them from any form of civil or criminal liability in respect of statements made by them in the *Oireachtas*. Court decisions have been very clear on the absolute privilege afforded to parliamentarians in the course of their duties by virtue of this provision. The corollary in Article 15.12 states that 'all official reports and publications of the *Oireachtas* ... and utterances made in either House wherever published shall be privileged'. This means that a media outlet which publishes a statement made in the *Oireachtas* would also be immune from civil or criminal liability. This provision has received little attention and while a case last year confirmed the immunity,[104] the Court did not take the opportunity to discuss the provision and therefore, we have never received a judicial explanation of the exact meaning of this esoteric phrase or the extent of protection afforded by it. In particular, it is not clear whether this is an absolute or a qualified privilege.

105. Article 15.10 also allows each House to create and administer its own rules and where these rules are broken, penalties may be imposed. Thus, while *Oireachtas* members have complete protection against any legal proceedings which might otherwise arise from speeches made in the *Oireachtas*, the *Dáil*'s standing orders attempt to offset this privilege by providing certain procedural safeguards. Standing Order 59 contains a right of reply for aggrieved persons who feel that their names have been unfairly tarnished by privileged utterances in the *Dáil*. In such cases, if the Committee on Procedure and Privileges feels that an abuse has indeed taken place, the official record of the House can be rebalanced and the offending remark can be expunged.

§3. Competence

106. According to Article 15.2.1°, the sole law making power in Ireland is vested in the *Oireachtas*. This Article is supplemented by Article 29.6, which prevents the implementation of any international agreement without the consent of the *Oireachtas*. However, in order to allow for the European Union to make law for Ireland, there is one significant exception; Article 29.4.6°, which effectively prevails over Article 15.2.1°.[105]

103. [1993] 3 IR 227.
104. *O'Brien v. Radio Telefis Eireann* [2015] IEHC 379.
105. *See* paras 21,22, 188.

107. The Houses have the power, by joint resolution, to remove various constitutional office holders such as the President, judges and the Attorney General. Legislation must be passed, or deemed to have been passed, by both Houses before being signed into law by the President. The declaration of a state of emergency, and its termination, must also be made by both Houses of the *Oireachtas*.

§4. Working

108. The Constitution grants superior power to the *Dáil* in the law-making process. While the *Seanad* may reject or delay a proposal, it cannot override a decision of the *Dáil*. Ordinarily, a bill will be first introduced into the *Dáil* (although bills can also be introduced into the *Seanad*). There it will go through five stages, during which time the bill is debated and amended and if passed, it is then sent on to the *Seanad*. The *Seanad* then has ninety days (or a longer period which may be agreed by both Houses) to consider the bill. The bill will go through the same five legislative stages in the *Seanad*. If the *Seanad* rejects a bill, or returns it to the *Dáil* with amendments that are unacceptable to the *Dáil*, the bill will lapse. However, within 180 days, the *Dáil* may pass a resolution which deems the bill to have been passed by both Houses. It will then proceed to the President for signature as normal. Therefore, the *Seanad* can delay but cannot prevent the enactment of legislation.[106]

109. The *Seanad* has even less power when it comes to 'Money Bills'. Article 22 defines a 'Money Bill' as:

> the imposition, repeal, remission, alteration or regulation of taxation; the imposition for the payment of debt or other financial purposes of charges on public moneys or the variation or repeal of any such charges; supply; the appropriation, receipt, custody, issue or audit of accounts of public money; the raising or guarantee of any loan or the repayment thereof; matters subordinate and incidental to these matters or any of them.

110. This type of bill may only be initiated in the *Dáil* and the extent of the power of the *Seanad* is to make 'recommendations'. If the *Seanad* does not make any recommendations within a period of twenty-one days, then the bill will be deemed to have passed through both Houses of the *Oireachtas*.

§5. Delegation of Legislative Power

111. While Article 15.2.1° provides that no other authority has the power to make legislation in Ireland, there is the possibility of subordinate or delegated legislation, provided certain criteria are satisfied. This subordinate legislation usually takes the form of a statutory instrument, which supplements detail in primary legislation. The

106. However, the Seanad can effectively block a bill by using the Article 27 procedure, urging the President not to sign a controversial bill into law. However, this eventuality has never actually occurred.

Supreme Court, in the case of *Cityview Press Ltd. v. An Comhairle Oiliúna*,[107] decided that the test to be applied when deciding whether a delegation of legislative power is constitutional or not is: 'whether that which is challenged ... is more than a mere giving effect to the principles and policies which are contained in the statute itself'. Therefore, a statutory instrument must only add to or develop the general principles and policies already contained in the primary legislation and it cannot change, amend or repeal an Act of the *Oireachtas*.

112. Statutory instruments are ministerial orders – in other words, they are executive ordinances. Hundreds of these orders are passed every year and while they usually relate to very small technical matters, there is some opposition to the idea of executive law-making. The principle objection is based on the idea of the Rule of Law; the idea that law should be definite and accessible. While primary legislation is conducted under public scrutiny, secondary or delegated legislation is often passed under relative obscurity. All that is required is that the instrument be 'laid before the House', which may simply mean entry into the parliamentary library. However, an outright ban on the making of statutory instruments would put incredible pressure on the parliamentary system and so this is why a compromise was reached in the *Cityview* case to allow for the making of delegated legislation in such a way that it does not offend Article 15.2.1°. In that and subsequent cases, the Courts have clarified that where the *Oireachtas* gives the power to make regulations to an administrative body (including a Minister), these bodies are not 'law makers' nor do they constitute 'subordinate legislatures'.

113. While the *Oireachtas* may delegate the function of adding detail to laws, it may not delegate the power to make, repeal or amend the law. As the Courts have pointed out, a regulation is no more than the mere putting into effect of the principles and policies of the *Oireachtas* as set out in the statute itself.

114. Delegated legislation is also used in order to implement many EU Directives. Unlike EU regulations which have direct effect and are immediately applicable in the domestic sphere, Member States retain discretion as to how Directives are implemented. Due in large part to the sheer volume of this kind of legislation, Ireland has chosen to implement most of this legislation by statutory instrument. The appropriateness of this method of implementing EU law was considered in the case of *Meagher v. Minister for Agriculture*.[108] This case centred on a Directive which had the effect of reducing the amount of weight-enhancing drugs farmers were allowed to give to their pigs. The statutory instrument, which implemented this Directive in Ireland, provided that a person could be prosecuted summarily for exceeding the specified dosage, and it also allowed a prosecution within two years of the offence. This had the effect of contradicting existing legislation; namely, The Petty Session Act 1851, which states generally that there must be a summary prosecution within six months. It was argued therefore that the means of implementing the Directive was unconstitutional as it was contrary to Article 15.2.1° and it did not satisfy the *Cityview* test since it purported to amend a piece of legislation, something known as a Henry VIII clause.[109] The Minister defended himself by invoking Article 29.4.6°. The farmer's response was that the Directive

107. [1980] IR 381.
108. [1994] 1 IRLM 1.
109. For more, *see* Neil Maddox, 'The Legality of Henry VIII Clauses' (2004) 9 (5) BR 188.

could have been implemented by a way of an Act of the *Oireachtas*; all that was necessitated by EU obligation was the content, as the EU is neutral regarding the form of law chosen to implement EU obligations. Consequently, it was not necessary to violate Article 15.2.1°. This argument succeeded before the High Court. However, the Supreme Court overturned this and accepted the Minister's final argument, that since the EU produces such a copious amount of legislation, if all or even most of it had to be into effect in Ireland by way of an Act of the Oireachtas, having to go through all the various legislative stages in both the *Dáil* and *Seanad*, there would be too much work for the *Oireachtas* to do and not enough time in which to do it. The acceptance by the Supreme Court of this argument has been criticized.

115. A second similar case followed in which the Court had the opportunity to clarify its reasoning. In *Maher v. Minister for Agriculture*,[110] the implementation of an EU Directive on milk quotas was challenged along the same lines as the previous case. However, the Supreme Court now indicated disquiet with its acceptance of the pragmatic argument based on the infeasibility of implementing all Directives as Acts of the *Oireachtas*. It stated that statutory instruments were not always an appropriate way of implementing EU law. However, the Supreme Court did find for the Minister on a different basis. The Court explained that what was required by Article 15.2.1° was that no new legal principle should be laid down in delegated legislation. This requirement could be satisfied, as it was in the present circumstances, by all the principles being contained in the Directive, rather than, as in previous cases, within an Act of the *Oireachtas*. Thus the Minister was doing no more than 'giving effect to the principles and policies' already contained within the Directive. It was stressed however, that if an EU measure was to leave certain policy matters to Member States to decide and if all such matters were not settled within the Directive itself, then a statutory instrument would not be the appropriate means of implementation and an Act of the *Oireachtas* would be needed.

110. [2001] 2 IR 139.

Chapter 4. The Executive

§1. The Organ of State

116. Article 28.2 provides that the executive power of the State is exercised by the Government. The Government consists of a Prime Minister, called the *Taoiseach*, a Deputy Prime Minister, called the *Tánaiste*, and between five and thirteen other Ministers. Normally the Government consists of fifteen members, including the *Taoiseach* and *Tánaiste*. The *Dáil* nominates the *Taoiseach*, usually the leader of the most successful Party at election, and then approves the other members of Government, who are then officially appointed by the President. Save occasionally in cases where there are a lot of Independents, the *Dáil* is merely the device by which the vote is formally registered. The President is also acting formally as it is effectively the *Taoiseach* who appoints the Ministers. The only limitation is that Ministers must be members of either House of the *Oireachtas* but no more than two Senators may be appointed. Also, according to Article 28.7.1°, the *Taoiseach*, *Tánaiste* and Minister for Finance must be members of the *Dáil*. In practice, all Ministers will usually be members of the *Dáil*.[111]

117. The *Taoiseach* is responsible for the running of the Government and is head of a Department. Unlike other ministerial portfolios, the Department of the *Taoiseach* is concerned with the coordination of policy across all other Departments. As well as nominating Ministers and eleven members of the *Seanad*, the Taoiseach also nominates the Attorney General, is a member of the Council of State and is responsible for keeping the President informed regarding matters of domestic and international policy. The *Taoiseach* also has the power to dismiss Ministers and can request a dissolution of the *Dáil* from the President.[112]

§2. Legal Status

I. Executive Privilege

118. In the past, it was taken for granted that the State had inherited this evidential rule from the United Kingdom. The rule forms part of the Royal Prerogative in the UK and means that the State does not have to disclose sensitive official documents in court. However, in the 1972 Supreme Court decision in *Murphy v. Dublin*,[113] this privilege was severely restricted. While the Court accepted that there is a public interest in maintaining the confidentiality of certain official documents, and this was justifiable

111. In very rare occasions, Senators have been appointed as Ministers.
112. As noted above, the President can only refuse to dissolve the *Dáil* if the *Taoiseach* has lost the support of the majority in the *Dáil*.
113. [1972] 2 IR 215.

on the basis of 'the public interest' and not connected to the Prerogative,[114] the position in England and Wales, whereby the responsible Minister decides whether the confidentiality of the document outweighs public interest in its disclosure, was rejected. Instead, it was held that it is for the Court to decide on a case-by-case basis whether or not sensitive official documents may be disclosed.

II. Collective Responsibility

119. Article 28.4.1° provides that the Government is responsible to the *Dáil* and as mentioned above, the *Taoiseach* and Government must resign on ceasing to command the support of the majority of the *Dáil*, although they remain in office until their successors are appointed. Article 24.4.2° requires that the Government meets and acts as a collective authority. In practice, this means that while a Minister might not necessarily agree with a decision made in Cabinet, this disagreement does not usually come to light. Instead decisions emanate from Cabinet with a single voice. David Gwynn Morgan has explained the advantages with collective responsibility:

> [I]t makes it more likely that there will be a stable Government which can rely on holding office usually for a period of years. Secondly, if each member of the Government knows that he may be called to account for the irresponsibility or poor judgment of his colleagues, such behaviour is more likely to be forestalled. Finally, it assists the clear expression of decisions and allocation of responsibility. But even without a collective responsibility convention, unity would usually be desirable in the Government's own interest, since a lack of public confidence is likely to be engendered if ministers are at loggerheads in public.[115]

120. The issue of collective responsibility has been thrown into focus in recent times due to the composition of the current administration and the fact that the Cabinet includes Independent Ministers, who do not always agree with government policy. In fact, in July 2016, three Independent Ministers voted for a private members bill, despite the fact that the Attorney General had advised that the bill would be unconstitutional and the Government had announced that it would not support the bill for this reason. While Ministers have resigned or been dismissed in the past due to disagreements with their colleagues in government, it appears there were no such consequences on this occasion. The problem with this rule is that it is not clear what exactly is required by the provision or when exactly it is broken or even whether there are sanctions for breach of the rule. As Morgan has pointed out, it is not a rule which can be enforced by the Courts as such. Rather it is more of a convention and thus, 'subject to the frailties … to which all conventions are prey.'[116]

114. In the same year, in the case of *Byrne v. Ireland* (n. 14), the Supreme Court decided the State had not inherited the Prerogative as it was inconsistent with the doctrine of popular sovereignty that is enshrined in the Irish Constitution.

115. Morgan (n. 15) 73.

116. *Ibid.*

III. Cabinet Confidentiality

121. In order to preserve the appearance of a united front and maintain the integrity of Government policies, it is necessary that there is confidentiality over discussions in Cabinet. This idea of confidentiality of Cabinet discussions, while not originally mentioned in the Constitution, was confirmed by the Supreme Court in *Attorney General v. Hamilton* (No. 1).[117] It was stated that to reveal the content of Cabinet meetings would possibly undermine the principle of collective responsibility required by Article 24.4.2°. However, it was felt that the rule as formulated by the *Hamilton* case was too rigid and so the Seventeenth Amendment was passed in 1997 in order to clarify the rule. The new Article 28.4.3° provides that the confidentiality of Government meetings shall be respected unless the High Court orders that a disclosure should be made on application by a court if shown to be in the interests of the administration of justice or on application by a tribunal of inquiry where there is an over-riding public interest in disclosure. Of course, sometimes it suits the Government to disregard the principle of confidentiality, for example very often details of upcoming Government policies are leaked to the media for political or strategic purposes.

IV. Individual Ministerial Responsibility

122. There is another aspect of responsibility to the *Dáil*, namely individual ministerial responsibility. This means that if a Minister commits some individual act of misconduct or dishonesty then he/she should either resign or be dismissed by the *Taoiseach*, or if neither happens, be removed by a *Dáil* resolution. This rule is not mentioned in the Constitution but is generally accepted to be a Convention of the Constitution. However, as a result of Party politics, the doctrine is not strictly adhered to. In practice, unless it relates to a personal indiscretion, the Government Party, which holds a majority in the *Dáil*, will support the Minister and therefore any motion of no confidence would be defeated. Therefore, while in theory, Ministers are expected to be individually responsible for their behaviour, very often the issue is turned into a matter of collective responsibility as the rest of the Ministers decide to close ranks in support of their colleague. If however, it is felt that the behaviour of the Minister has been politically damaging or that it would be damaging to the Government or the Party to the support the Minister, then the Minister will usually have to fall on his/her own sword.

§3. Competence

123. Article 28.2 provides that the executive power of the State is to be exercised by or on the authority of the Government. However, the Constitution does not elaborate on the meaning of the words 'executive power'. Later in Articles 29.4.1° and 49.2, we are told that external relations comes within the remit of executive power and that the exercise of all powers, functions, rights and prerogatives formerly exercisable in respect

117. [1993] 2 IR 250.

of *Saorstát Éireann* also come within that remit. Other than these directions, the Constitution is silent as to the extent of executive power. In fact, Professor Casey has pointed out that the impression given by a literal reading of the Constitution is 'seriously misleading'[118] in that there are many other powers which are actually exercised by the Government. In the case of *Haughey v. Moriarty*,[119] Chief Justice Hamilton stated that: 'the powers of the organs of government are not restricted to those expressly set forth in the Constitution but rather include the powers normally exercised by such organs in a sovereign and democratic state.'

I. International Affairs

124. As noted above, the Constitution specifically directs that the Government exercises executive power with regard to the area of external or international affairs. The Supreme Court decided in the case of *Crotty v. An Taoiseach*[120] that the exercise of this power is subject to judicial review. Yet the Courts will only interfere with the exercise of such executive powers where 'the circumstances are such as to amount to a clear disregard by the Government of the powers and duties conferred upon it by the Constitution.'[121]

II. Financial Affairs

125. While it is not specifically enumerated in the Constitution, one of the central executive powers of the Government is to manage the financial affairs of the State. While Article 28.4.4° does provide that the Government 'shall prepare Estimates of the Receipts and Estimates of the State for each financial year, and shall present them to *Dáil Éireann* for consideration', the reality is that the Government has a much stronger role than the Article would suggest. Article 17.2 emphasizes the Government's dominance over the *Dáil* in this area by providing that the *Dáil* shall not pass any vote or resolution or enact any law for the appropriation of public moneys unless it has been approved by the Government and signed by the *Taoiseach*. Thus it is the executive which initiates financial action; this is then usually approved by the *Oireachtas* and supervised by the Comptroller and Auditor General.[122]

III. Other Executive Powers

126. While, the Constitution also confers certain powers on the Government as a whole, such as nominating judges, many other powers are conferred upon it by statute. These include powers such as the creation of special courts and the appointment

118. Casey, (n. 84) 230-231.
119. [1999] 3 IR 1.
120. *Crotty* (n. 16).
121. *Boland v. An Taoiseach* [1974] IR 338.
122. *See* paras 169–170.

of various office holders.[123] However, in practice it will be the creation of policy rather than the exercise of formal legal powers which will occupy much of the time of the Cabinet. In addition, while technically the work of creating legislation is the task and preserve of the *Oireachtas*, due to the level of control exercised by the Government over the *Oireachtas*, legislation is usually developed initially at Cabinet level.

§4. Working

I. General Working

127. The Constitution does not elaborate on the actual workings of the executive. However, practices have developed, some of which are now outlined in legislation. The Government usually meets for a Cabinet meeting once a week on a Tuesday morning. Although the term 'Cabinet' does not appear in the Constitution, it is frequently used to describe formal meetings of the Government, to distinguish them from more general activities of government. As outlined above, the proceedings of Cabinet meetings are confidential. These meetings include business such as the exercise of formal powers, i.e. advising the President to exercise specific powers, considering and approving major policy issues and making Orders to give effect to statutory provisions.

128. Article 28.12 provides that the distribution of business among 'Departments of State' as well as the designation of members of Government to be the Ministers in charge of those Departments shall be regulated by statute. The roles and duties of ministers are set out in The Ministers and Secretaries Acts, 1924-2013. The original Act, while it has been amended on many occasions, provides the basic framework that is still followed today. Under this legislation, each minister is made a corporation sole. Departments may also have a Minister of State or Junior Minister. These Ministers are appointed by the Government on the nomination of the *Taoiseach* and must be members of the *Oireachtas*. Under Article 28.8, Government Ministers (though not Junior Ministers[124]) have the right to speak and attend either House of the *Oireachtas*, although they can only vote in the House to which they belong.

123. *See* Casey (n. 84) 160.

124. Junior Ministers are non-Cabinet Ministers who are appointed by the Cabinet on the nomination of the Taoiseach and are usually attached to one or more Departments of State. They are sometimes referred to as Ministers of State. The posts were created by The Ministers and Secretaries (Amendment) (No. 2) Act, 1977, which provides that a Minister of State may be delegated a power or duty by the Minister of the Government they support. In the original Act the number of Ministers of State was limited to 10, but in 1980 this was raised to 15, in 1995 it was raised to 17, and in 2007 it was raised to twenty. The current administration includes fifteen Junior Ministers. Certain Junior Ministers are referred to as 'Super' Junior Ministers – this means that they may attend Cabinet meetings but are not permitted to vote.

II. Government Control of the Dáil

129. While, as outlined above, the Constitution provides that the Government shall be responsible to the *Dáil*, in reality, the Government controls the *Dáil*. This is so because of the particular party structure in Ireland whereby the Government comprises the central figures of the majority party in the *Dáil* (and any minor coalition partner). Therefore, the other party members in the *Dáil* will be forced to 'toe the party line' by use of the whip system. Even when the Government parties may not have a stable majority, this can usually be attained through the support of Independent Deputies. Many Independents who have supported Governments were themselves previously former members of that party.

In the past, this level of control was exemplified by the fact that the *Ceann Comhairle* (chairperson of the *Dáil*) was always effectively chosen by the Government party (or parties),[125] as well as the fact that the Government sets the *Dáil* agenda and chooses the chairs for the majority of *Dáil* committees.[126] However, as part of a recent reform, the election of the *Ceann Comhairle* was changed to a secret ballot with the result that a member of the Opposition was elected. (This is due to the particular political scenario whereby the Government of the day does not have a stable majority in the *Dáil* and the biggest Opposition Party has made a pact to support the Government.)

130. The whip system is also used to great effect in order to ensure that the Government will win any *Dáil* vote on legislation. The result of this rigid system of party discipline is that the *Dáil* will almost never vote against a Government decision. Because of the way in which members of the *Seanad* are chosen, it is also normal for Government parties to hold a concurrent majority in the *Seanad*, which also ensures Government support in the Upper House. The control exercised by the Government over the *Oireachtas*, has led to the description of this system as a fused executive-legislature.

131. Due to the current dissatisfaction with Party politics in Ireland and the subsequent rise of Independent Deputies, which has led to the current situation where the Government was unable to form a stable majority and has had to rely upon an Opposition pact, reform has been proposed in order to make the Government more responsible to the *Dáil* and thus to bring practice more in line with the level of power separation actually expected in the Constitution.

---

125. While, officially the *Ceann Comhairle* was elected by an 'open ballot' of all TDs currently sitting in the *Dáil* at that time, due to the level of control exercised by party leaders, the preferred candidate of the majority party would always win this vote, thereby effectively allowing the Government of the day to select the *Ceann Comhairle*.

126. Except for those few committees, such as the Public Accounts Committee, which are chaired by opposition TDs.

Chapter 5. The Judiciary

§1. Introduction

132. Articles 34 to 37 deal with the Courts and the Judiciary. They follow the same basic arrangement which had originally been provided for under the 1922 Constitution. Articles 64 to 73 of the 1922 document set out a basic unitary structure and The Courts of Justice Act 1924 provided the detail for the establishment and jurisdiction of a Supreme Court, Court of Criminal Appeal, High Court, Circuit Court, and District Court. The current 1937 Constitution retains this structure but it was decided by the Supreme Court in the case of *State (Keegan) v. Minister for Justice*,[127] that it was necessary to re-establish the courts system with new legislation under the new Constitution. The Courts (Establishment and Constitution) Act 1961 was then passed, which provided for the continuation of the existing court system but which also updated and provided clarification on the system. The most recent change to the system was an amendment to the Constitution in 2013 to provide for a permanent Court of Appeal, dealing with civil as well as criminal matters.

133. Article 34.1 declares that justice 'shall be administered in courts established by law by judges appointed in the manner provided by this Constitution'. This has been interpreted to mean that only judges can exercise the 'administration of justice' function. This has two principal consequences: first, it means that neither the executive nor the legislature can interfere with the courts' adjudicating functions; second, it means that bodies, other than courts, may not exercise functions which are deemed to constitute the 'administration of justice'. This phrase was considered in the case of *McDonald v. Bord na gCon* (no. 2)[128] and was said usually to involve the following characteristics:

(1) a dispute or controversy as to the existence of legal rights or a violation of the law;
(2) a determination or ascertainment of the rights of the parties of the imposition of liabilities or the infliction of a penalty;
(3) the final determination (subject to appeal) of legal rights or liabilities or the imposition of penalties;
(4) the enforcement of those rights or liabilities or the imposition of a penalty by the Court or by the executive power of the State which is called on by the Court to enforce its judgment; and
(5) the making of an order by the Court which, as a matter of history is an order characteristic of courts in this country.

134. Therefore, it is normally held that any extra-judicial body or organization, whose functions involve all of these features, is unconstitutionally exercising the

127. [1954] IR 207.
128. [1965] IR 217.

administration of justice. There are exceptions however, as Article 37.1 allows for the exercise of certain 'limited' functions and powers of a judicial nature. This is to allow for quasi-judicial bodies such as tribunals, disciplinary bodies and certain administrative organizations to carry out functions similar to those exercised by judges. However, in order to be constitutional, the functions must be 'limited' and cannot deal with criminal matters.[129]

135. Article 34.1 also declares that justice is to be administered in public. This is seen as necessary in order to preserve public confidence in the administration of justice. However, the Constitution does allow for certain limited exceptions to be provided by statute. Matters such as child custody, divorce, the protection of trade secrets, lunacy and urgent applications for *habeas corpus* are often held *in camera*.

§2. Organization

I. Ordinary Courts

136. The structure of the courts in Ireland is a unitary one, with most of the courts exercising a civil as well as a criminal jurisdiction. The Constitution specifically provides for the High Court, Supreme Court and since 2013, the Court of Appeal, and envisages that courts of 'local and limited jurisdiction' will be provided for. Article 34.2 also specifies that the courts shall comprise both courts of first instance and a court of final appeal.

A. The Supreme Court

137. The Supreme Court is the court of final appeal. It has original jurisdiction in only two specific instances; under Article 12.3, it has the power to determine the incapacity of the President and under Article 26, it has the power to consider the constitutionality of a Bill before it becomes law.[130] The Court currently has nine sitting judges, including the Chief Justice. The President of the Court of Appeal and the President of the High Court are ex officio members of the Court. Normally, the Supreme Court sits in divisions of three or five judges and, in exceptional circumstances, seven judges. When hearing cases concerning the constitutional validity of an Act of the *Oireachtas*, the Constitution requires that the court consists of a minimum of five judges. This requirement also applies for an Article 26 reference and for a determination of the capacity of the President under Article 12.3.

138. The Supreme Court exercises appellate jurisdiction from a decision of the Court of Appeal if the Supreme Court is satisfied that the decision involves a matter of general public importance, or if it is necessary in the interests of justice and from a decision of the High Court if satisfied that there are exceptional circumstances warranting a direct appeal to it. Article 34.4.5° also provides that no law may be enacted

129. *See for example* the case of *Re Solicitors Act* [1960] IR 239 where the Court outlined in detail what a 'limited' function should entail.

130. *See* paras 82–85.

excepting from the appellate jurisdiction of the Supreme Court, cases which involve questions as to the validity of any law having regard to the provisions of the Constitution. Accordingly, the Supreme Court is the final arbiter when interpreting the Constitution. This is significant, particularly given the power of judicial review exercised by the courts in Ireland.[131] Such cases must be brought in the first instance in the High Court but an appeal is available to the Court of Appeal and the Supreme Court.

B. The Court of Appeal

139. The Court of Appeal was established in October 2014 in order to provide an additional level between the High Court and the Supreme Court. The Court comprises a President and nine ordinary judges. The Chief Justice and the President of the High Court are ex officio members. It usually sits in divisions of three judges. Some interlocutory and procedural applications may be heard by a single judge. The Court has jurisdiction to hear appeals in civil proceedings from the High Court and in criminal proceedings from the Circuit Court, the Central Criminal Court and the Special Criminal Court.

C. The High Court

140. The High Court is the main Court of First Instance and according to Article 34.3, has full original jurisdiction to determine all judicial matters, whether of law or fact, civil or criminal. As well as dealing with everyday civil and criminal disputes, it is also the first instance court for determining most constitutional issues. The High Court also acts as an appeal court from the Circuit Court in civil matters and has the power to review the decisions of certain tribunals. The Court comprises the President and thirty-six ordinary judges. The President of the Circuit Court and the Chief Justice are, by virtue of their office, additional judges of the High Court. Proceedings are usually heard and determined by one judge only but the President of the High Court may decide that a case be heard by a divisional court of three judges.

D. The Central Criminal Court

141. The High Court, when exercising its criminal jurisdiction is known as the Central Criminal Court.

E. The Circuit Court

142. The Circuit Court was originally established by The Courts of Justice Act 1924 and formally re-established by The Courts (Establishment and Constitution) Act 1961. Article 34.3.4° makes it clear that such a court cannot have 'full' jurisdiction, therefore it is a court of 'local and limited' jurisdiction. The Circuit Court consists of the President, thirty-seven ordinary judges and six specialist judges. The President of the District Court is, by virtue of his/her office, an additional judge of the Circuit Court. The country is divided into eight circuits, with one judge assigned to each circuit with

131. *See* paras 160–162.

the exception of Dublin and Cork, where additional judges are assigned due to the population size in these circuits. In criminal matters the Circuit Court has the same jurisdiction as the Central Criminal Court in all indictable offences except murder, rape, aggravated sexual assault, treason, piracy and related offences. The civil jurisdiction of the Circuit Court is a limited one unless all parties to an action consent, in which case the jurisdiction is unlimited. The limit is set by legislation. Decisions of the District Court can be appealed to the Circuit Court with some exceptions.[132] Appeals proceed by way of a full rehearing and the decision of the Circuit Court is final.

F. The District Court

143. The District Court is the lowest court in the hierarchy and was also established by legislation. It is a court of local and summary jurisdiction. The Court is made up of a President and sixty-three ordinary judges. The country is divided into twenty-three districts, with one or more judges permanently assigned to each district. The District Court handles a large number of cases, mainly in matters of criminal, civil, family and licensing law. The Court is empowered to hear and determine minor criminal matters. Its civil jurisdiction is based on a monetary limit set by legislation. It has a wide jurisdiction in family law and considers matters such as safety and barring orders, guardianship of children, maintenance and child care orders. The District Court also has wide powers in relation to liquor and lottery licensing. The Court also deals with miscellaneous matters such as actions taken under The Control of Dogs Acts, applications for citizenship, applications to amend birth and marriage certificates etc.

II. Special Courts

A. Special Criminal Court

144. Article 38.3.1° provides for the establishment of special courts by legislation where it is determined that 'the ordinary courts are inadequate to secure the effective administration of justice and the preservation of public peace and order.' The Special Criminal Court was established by The Offences Against the State Act 1939. The main feature of the Court is that instead of a jury, the accused is tried before three judges, from a panel of eleven, drawn from the High, Circuit and District Courts. The rules of evidence that apply in proceedings before the Special Criminal Court are the same as those applicable to trials in the Central Criminal Court. Cases are transferred from the ordinary criminal courts to the Special Criminal Court if the offence involved is a scheduled offence or if the Director of Public Prosecutions issues a certificate stating that in his/her opinion, the ordinary courts are inadequate to secure the administration of justice and the preservation of public peace and order. Scheduled offences generally involve subversive crime and are automatically transferred to the Special Criminal Court. The current list of scheduled offences includes: offences under The Explosive

132. The Circuit Court also acts as an appeal court for appeals from the decisions of certain administrative bodies and tribunals such as the Labour Court, Unfair Dismissals Tribunal and the Employment Appeals Tribunal.

Substances Act 1883; offences under The Firearms Acts 1925 to 2006; offences under The Offences against the State Acts 1939 to 1998; offences under Part 7 of The Criminal Justice Act 2006 (excluding conspiracy).An appeal against any conviction or sentence from a Special Criminal Court may be taken to the Court of Appeal.

B. The Children Court

145. The Children Court was established by The Children Act 2001 and deals with children under the age of 18 years. The idea was to separate these cases from the ordinary sittings involving adults and while such cases also take place in the District Court, they usually occur in a different room or during a different day or time to the ordinary sittings. While certain offences such as manslaughter must be held in the Central Criminal Court, the Children Court may deal with most other offences.

§3. Judicial Independence

146. Article 35.2 declares that 'All judges shall be independent in the exercise of their judicial functions and subject only to this Constitution and the law.' This is considered to be a central feature of the Irish Constitutional structure. It means that judges must be independent of the executive and legislature but also of any parties appearing before them. Moreover, it means that neither the executive nor the legislature may act in a manner which jeopardizes judicial independence.

147. In order to preserve this independence, the Constitution provides that judges are not eligible for membership of either House of the *Oireachtas* nor can they hold any other paid office. Their pay is also protected by Article 35.5[133] and they can only be removed by resolutions in the *Dáil* and the *Seanad.* Under the Common Law, judges are also immune from liability for acts done in the performance of their judicial duties. In the case of *Coyle v. Roe,*[134] Hamilton J. described this rule as 'absolute and universal'. The immunity applies even where the judge is unknowingly acting in excess of jurisdiction.

148. However, Hogan and Whyte have noted that 'the independence of the courts and their immunity from control by the *Oireachtas* is not absolute and could scarcely be made so.'[135] They reference the fact that the court structure and court procedure are ultimately prescribed by statute and open to change by the *Oireachtas.* They also point out that there is nothing to prevent the *Oireachtas* from passing a law to nullify the future effect of a court's judgment. They warn that 'the position of the judges is not quite as impregnable as a casual reading of ... Article 35 might suggest' but they concede that the actual judicial process itself does appear to be inviolable. Furthermore, the practice in Ireland has always been to fiercely protect judicial independence – judges are careful to distance themselves from the other branches of government and in general, the other branches are very respectful of the judicial arm.

133. *See* paras 158–159 on Remuneration.
134. Irish Times (Dublin, 26 Jun. 1984).
135. Hogan & Whyte (n. 9) 663.

According to recent EU surveys, the Irish legal system was ranked very high for its perceived level of judicial independence.[136]

§4. Appointment, Tenure, Removal and Remuneration of Judges

I. Appointment

149. Article 35.1 states that: 'The judges of the Supreme Court, the High Court and all other Courts established in pursuance of Article 34 hereof shall be appointed by the President.' However, as noted above, the role of the President is merely a ceremonial one, as in accordance with Article 13.9, this function is to be exercised 'only on the advice of the Government'. Thus, judges in Ireland are effectively appointed by the Government.

150. In the past, the process was quite informal. Indeed, the All Party *Oireachtas* Committee on the Constitution described how 'successive Governments were seen to appoint almost invariably, their own supporters to judicial office.'[137] Then in 1995, in response to the fallout from the attempted appointment of the then Attorney General to the post of President of the High Court,[138] the Judicial Appointments Advisory Board (JAAB) was established under The Courts and Court Officers Act, 1995 in order to provide a fair and impartial system for appointing judges. Section 16(2) of the Act, requires the JAAB to recommend to the Minister for Justice at least seven persons for appointment to a particular post. Although the 1995 Act empowers the JAAB to arrange for the interviewing of candidates, the JAAB has chosen not to exercise this power. Section 14(2)(f) also provides that the JAAB can do such other things as it considers necessary to enable it to discharge its functions under this Act. While the Act does bestow wide powers on the JAAB, the body has been very cautious in exercising its functions, in a misguided attempt to avoid unconstitutionally usurping the role of the Government in appointing judges. However, this caution is unnecessary as all that the Constitution requires is that the Government appoints judges. Therefore narrowing down the prospective pool of candidates to seven, (or even three as is currently proposed by many interest groups) would not constitute an unconstitutional usurpation of executive power.

151. It was recently decided to conduct a review of the judicial appointment process, with a view to reform. This is because of criticism that the current process is often seen as being political – with Governments appointing their own supporters to judicial office. As well as this, the process does nothing to encourage a diverse judiciary. In fact, while recent years have seen improvements, the Irish judiciary is quite a homogenous group; mainly male, white and upper-middle class. Furthermore, there are issues with the JAAB itself: First, the board has no role if the post in question is

136. The EU Justice Scoreboard is available at http://ec.europa.eu/justice/effective-justice/scoreboard/index_en.htm. Although Ireland was ranked second in 2014, by 2016 it had slipped to fifth.

137. All Party Oireachtas Committee on the Constitution, *Fourth Progress Report: The Courts and the Judiciary* (Stationary Office, 1999) 7.

138. For more on this *see* David Morgan, 'Selection of Superior Judges' (2004) 22 I.L.T. 42.

the presidency of any court or if a vacancy is being filled by the promotion of a lower judge by the Government. The second problem is that while it is clearly intended to be an advisory body, the JAAB is in fact nothing more than a filtering mechanism or short-listing aid whereby undesirable or unqualified candidates are excluded. The requirement that at least seven names be recommended and the fact that candidates are not interviewed or assessed in any formal manner means that in reality, there is nothing 'advisory' about the process. The Department of Justice initiated a consultation process on possible reforms in 2014 and has committed to publishing a bill in 2017.

II. Tenure and Removal

152. The retirement age of judges is regulated by statute. Under The Courts and Court Officers Act 1995, the retirement age of Supreme Court and High Court judges was reduced from 72 years to 70 years.[139] This brings them in line with Circuit Court judges, who also retire at the age of 70. District Court judges retire at the lower age of 65 years.

153. The Constitution provides for security of tenure for superior court judges only, with Article 35.4.1° stating that judges of these courts 'shall not be removed from office except for stated misbehaviour or incapacity'. Circuit and District Court judges are also subject to the same arrangement by legislation. Thus, while the removal process for lower court judges could technically be amended by a simple Act of the *Oireachtas*, it is highly unlikely at this stage that any distinction could reasonably be made between the process for lower and superior court judges. In fact, the original distinction between lower and superior court judges was principally made for historical reasons, when judges of the lower courts were often not professional judges and it was felt that more protection should be afforded to the professional superior court judges.

154. The removal process itself is very vague. Article 35.4 simply states that resolutions should be passed by the *Dáil* and *Seanad* calling for the judge's removal. When this is done the *Taoiseach* should then notify the President who, 'by an order under his hand and seal' will remove the judge from office. This Article stands in marked contrast to the procedure outlined in Article 12 which sets out a detailed impeachment procedure for the President. In fact, the lack of detail provided for the removal of a member of the judiciary from office has caused difficulties, most notably in the single case in which it was attempted to remove a judge in Ireland.

155. In January 2003, former Circuit Court judge Brian Curtin was charged with possession of child pornography. Evidence had been found on his computer, which had been seized as part of a *Garda* (Police) operation. However, the evidence could not be used as the warrant had expired by the time the search was carried out by *Gardaí* and Curtin was subsequently acquitted. Following an outburst of public anger and a refusal by the judge to voluntarily step down, an impeachment motion was moved in the *Dáil*. The *Dáil* suspended the motion and established a joint *Oireachtas*

---

139. Judges appointed prior to the coming into operation of that Act may continue in office until they reach the age of 72. Also, judges who previously held other judicial offices before being appointed to either the High or Supreme Courts may remain on in their respective judicial role until they reach the age of 72.

committee to examine the evidence and report back. This inquiry was challenged by Judge Curtin. The Supreme Court ruling in March 2006 upheld the process but gave a number of recommendations in order to ensure fair procedures. In November 2006, days before he was to give evidence to the committee, (and days after he had completed five years on the bench, the minimum required to qualify for a pension) Judge Curtin resigned on health grounds. The episode highlighted a number of problems in the process for removing judges. However, the Supreme Court ruling has, at least, provided some guidance for the future.

156. While there is no lesser form of discipline available for most judges in Ireland, beyond the nuclear option of removal, District Court judges occupy an unusual position in that there are specific statutory provisions providing for informal disciplinary measures. However, even these measures simply consist of a private enquiry and the possibility of the Chief Justice informing the wayward judge that their conduct has been such as to 'bring the administration of justice into disrepute.'

157. Various reports have been carried out with a view to reforming the system of judicial discipline and removal in Ireland.[140] The general consensus was that a Judicial Council should be established, which would have the power to consider complaints from the public, inquire into the behaviour of judges and issue sanctions. The majority of the reports favoured moral over legal sanctions, in order to preserve the integrity of the judge. In the years following the Curtin case, attempts were made to draw up legislation which would establish such a council. However, disagreements between the office of the Attorney General and the judiciary delayed the process. A draft Bill was then published in 2010, shortly before a general election. The election brought in a new Government, which gave a commitment to advance the Bill. A further general election was held in 2016 but no further progress has been made.

III. Remuneration

158. Article 35.5 specifies that 'the remuneration of a judge shall not be reduced during his continuance in office'. This is part of the protection of judicial independence and appears to rule out any attempt to manipulate a judge by reducing or threatening to reduce his remuneration. However, the provision has been the subject of some controversy. In the case of *O'Byrne v. Minister for Finance*,[141] a judge's widow argued that since her husband's salary had been reduced by the payment of income tax, the provision was violated. The Supreme Court, in deciding against her, took a purposive approach and explained that 'a judge who was subject to removal or to have his salary reduced would be under temptation to be subservient' and any discrimination by tax or against a judge or judges as a body, having the effect of reducing his salary, would be equally objectionable. However, it was stressed that a tax which is non-discriminatory against judges does not violate the provision. Moreover, the provision was not intended to give judges a more favourable position than other public servants.

140. *See* Laura Cahillane, 'Ireland's System for Disciplining and Removing Judges' (2015) 38 Dublin University Law Journal 55.
141. [1959] IR 1.

159. This issue caused controversy again in 2011, when the Government exempted the judiciary from a spate of public pay-cuts on the overly-cautious basis that the Constitution precludes a reduction in the salaries of judges and then proposed a constitutional amendment in order to remedy the situation. In a largely senseless measure, given the Supreme Court's very comprehensive ruling in the *O'Byrne*[142] case, the public voted in November 2011 to insert two sub-paragraphs into Article 35.5 which provide that the remuneration of judges is generally subject to the imposition of taxes, levies or other charges and that where reductions have been made to the pay of public servants in the public interest, proportionate reductions may also be made to the remuneration of judges.

§5. Judicial Review

160. There are two different procedures whereby the constitutionality of legislation may be decided by the Courts. The first is the Article 26 procedure, whereby the President may request the Supreme Court to consider whether a bill is consistent with the Constitution before it is passed into law.[143] The second procedure is provided by Article 34.3.2°, which gives the power of judicial review of legislation to the High Court. While in principle, this power is only available through this Article for laws enacted after the coming into force of the Constitution in 1937, Article 50 provides for the continuation of any pre-1937 laws which are not inconsistent with the Constitution and by virtue of Article 34.3.1°, the jurisdiction of the High Court extends to the question of whether a pre-1937 law is consistent. Thus, effectively both pre- and post-1937 laws can be challenged.

161. This power, which can be exercised by the High Court (and on appeal by the Court of Appeal and the Supreme Court), means that if a piece of legislation is found to infringe a constitutional provision, the offending provision will be struck down and held to be void *ab initio*. When the Court is considering such a challenge, it must apply the presumption of constitutionality. This presumption means that the burden of proof is on the party asserting the unconstitutionality and is based on Article 15.4.1°, which provides that the *Oireachtas* may not pass unconstitutional legislation. As a consequence, all legislation is thereby presumed by the courts to be consistent with the Constitution until proven otherwise.

162. Before 2013, any judgment emanating from the Supreme Court regarding the constitutionality of a law would have to be issued as a single, unanimous judgment. This rule was inserted into the Constitution by The Second Amendment of the Constitution Act 1941, in response to the judgment of the Supreme Court in the case of *Re Article 26 and the Offences Against the State (Amendment) Bill 1940*.[144] While the constitutionality of that particular Bill was upheld, when giving judgment for the Court, Chief Justice O'Sullivan announced that it was the judgment of a majority of the judges, implying that there had not been a consensus. For reasons of clarity and in order to obtain a definitive decision, it was then decided that all such subsequent

142. *Ibid.*
143. *See* paras 82–85 on Article 26 procedure.
144. [1940] IR 470.

judgments should have the appearance of unanimity, in order to provide certainty in the law. However, as part of the referendum to establish a new Court of Appeal in October 2013, the people voted to remove this rule from Article 34. Therefore, judges can now give dissenting opinions regarding the constitutionality of a law. However, the rule persists in Article 26.2.2° for decisions from the Supreme Court on a reference from the President.[145]

145. *Ibid.*

Chapter 6. Independent Non-political Agencies

§1. The Attorney General

I. The Office of Attorney General

163. Although the Attorney General was not mentioned in the Irish Free State Constitution of 1922, the Office of Attorney General has existed since the foundation of the State. The Ministers and Secretaries Act, 1924 gave the office some post-independence legislative grounding, charging the Attorney with representing the State in legal actions, prosecuting offences and the duty of advising the Government in matters of law and legal opinion. Article 30 of *Bunreacht na hÉireann* sets out the constitutional position of the Attorney General. There have been few changes to the role as set out in the 1924 Act, which is still in force and still provides the detail to complement the constitutional position. Article 30 confirms that the holder is 'the advisor to the Government in matters of law and legal opinion' and a number of additional roles and responsibilities were created for the Attorney under the Constitution, including his/her membership of the Council of State.[146] While the Attorney General sits in on cabinet meetings as an advisor, Article 30.4 makes it clear that he/she is not a member of the Government.

164. The Attorney General is appointed by the *Taoiseach*, who also has the power to remove her, and she must retire from office upon the resignation of the *Taoiseach*. Thus, usually the person appointed to the office will be someone associated with the political party currently in power. Neither the Constitution, nor the legislation specifies any particular qualification for the office of the Attorney General but the convention is to appoint a Senior Council. The Office of the Attorney General also comprises the Advisory Counsel to the Attorney General, the Office of Parliamentary Counsel (which provides most of the legislative drafting for Government-sponsored bills) as well as the Chief State Solicitor's Office (which provides litigation, conveyancing and other transactional services to the government).

II. Roles and Duties

165. The Attorney General advises the Government of the day on constitutional and legal issues, including whether proposed legislation complies with the provisions of the Constitution, acts and treaties of the European Union, the European Convention on Human Rights and any other international treaties to which Ireland has acceded.

166. The Attorney General is also the representative of the public in all legal proceedings for the enforcement of law and the assertion or protection of public rights

146. *See* paras 92–93.

and is sometimes referred to as 'Guardian of the Public Interest.'[147] While not specifically described as such in the Constitution, which concentrates on the Attorney General's role as legal advisor to the Government, section 6 of the 1924 Act makes this clear. However, this can sometimes lead to conflict, as this responsibility for upholding the public interest may at times be at odds with Government policy. Because of the potential for conflict here, the fact that the Attorney General is independent and not a member of Government is essential. Thus, despite the control exercised by the *Taoiseach* over the tenure of the Attorney General, it has been emphasized by the Courts that the office is independent of Government. The reality of this position means that, albeit on rare occasions, at times the Attorney may take action independently and against the wishes of the Government, for example in order to uphold a constitutional right, as happened in the case of *Attorney General v. X.*[148]

167. The Attorney General defends the constitutionality of bills referred to the Supreme Court under Article 26 of the Constitution and, as mentioned above, is an ex officio member of the Council of State which the President can consult in relation to the exercise of his Article 26 and other powers. The Attorney General also has functions in respect of the Law Reform Commission, under The Coroners Act 1962 (to direct a coroner to hold an inquest where she considers that the circumstances of a person's death make the holding of an inquest advisable), as well as some limited statutory functions, for example under The Geneva Conventions Act 1962.

168. Originally, the Attorney General was also responsible for the prosecution of all serious offences but Article 30.3 also envisages that this function may be carried out by 'some other person authorized by law'. So, in 1974, due to the heavy workload of the Attorney General, this function was transferred to the newly created office of the Director of Public Prosecutions.[149] In certain cases, criminal matters can be transferred back to the Attorney General, for example where the Government is of the opinion that it is 'expedient in the interests of national security'.

II. The Comptroller and Auditor General

169. Article 33, which substantially reproduces Articles 62 and 63 of the 1922 Constitution, provides that the functions of the Comptroller and Auditor General are 'to control on behalf of the State all disbursements and to audit all accounts of moneys

147. *See* Forde and Leonard (n. 18) 142.

148. In *AG. v. X* [1992] 1 IR 1, the Attorney General sought an injunction to prevent a young girl from travelling to the UK to procure an abortion. This was because of the importance accorded to the 'right to life of the unborn' under Article 40.3.3. While some members of the Government disapproved of such action and the injunction was ultimately not granted, the Supreme Court agreed that the Attorney General must act independently of the Government and was well within his rights to take such a case.

149. The Prosecution of Offences Act 1974. The Director of Public Prosecutions enforces the criminal law in the courts on behalf of the People of Ireland. She directs and supervises public prosecutions on indictment in the courts and gives general direction and advice to the Garda Síochána in relation to summary cases and specific direction in such cases where requested. The Chief Prosecution Solicitor provides a solicitor service, within the Office of the Director of Public Prosecutions, to act on behalf of the Director.

administered by or under the authority of the *Oireachtas.*' Further details are provided by The Comptroller and Auditor General Acts 1866-1998. Under the 1993 Act, the Comptroller is required to report to the *Dáil* in respect of certain matters including following the completion of the audit of appropriation accounts of the previous year and in respect of non-compliance with the Acts. The Comptroller also has power, under the 1998 Act, to carry out an investigation into the financial records of any State or State-sponsored body falling within the remit of the body, upon a request by the *Dáil.*

170. The office-holder is appointed by the President on the nomination of the *Dáil* and is given the same tenure as judges of the superior courts, i.e. is only removable for stated misbehaviour or incapacity and upon resolutions made by both Houses of the *Oireachtas*.

Part III. The State and Its Subdivisions

Chapter 1. State Form

§1. The State

171. As noted in the General Introduction section, 'Ireland' refers to the twenty-six counties that make up the Republic of Ireland. The remaining six counties of Northern Ireland are part of the United Kingdom. The island of Ireland covers 84,415 sq. km and out of this, the Republic of Ireland covers 70,283 sq. km. The country is divided into four provinces: Munster, Leinster, Connaught, and Ulster. This division is only for geographic, cultural and historical reasons however, as the provinces have no basis in law. The division into twenty-six counties is for administrative reasons; there are no federal elements in the country. Each county has its own county council, which exercises limited powers in relation to issues such as housing, planning, environmental protection, provision of recreational amenities and community infrastructure, etc.

172. The county councils do not correspond with the parliamentary electoral constituencies, of which there are forty. Article 16.2 stipulates that the number of members shall from time to time be fixed by law, but the total number of members of *Dáil Éireann* shall not be fixed at less than one member per 30,000 of the population, or at more than one member per 20,000 of the population. Figures are taken from the most up-to-date census information and Article 16.4 requires that the *Oireachtas* revise the constituencies at least once every twelve years, with due regard to changes in distribution of population.

173. Ireland is a mainly centralized, unitary State. However, provision is made in the Constitution under Article 15.2.2° for the creation and recognition of subordinate legislatures. This Article is a relic of the 1922 Constitution and was included in both Constitutions to provide for a possible future reunification of the North and South of Ireland.

174. The Constitution refers to the 'People', the 'Nation' and the 'State' in various different provisions. While the 'Nation' is difficult to define and sometimes appears to be a synonym for the 'People', the 'State' has a different meaning. While it is not actually specified in the Constitution, the 'State' seems to refer to the new entity created by the 1937 Constitution. In the case of *Commissioners of Public Works v. Kavanagh*,[150] Justice O'Dálaigh stated that 'in 1937 *Saorstát Éireann* was supplanted by the new State under the Constitution of Ireland.' In various different Articles, the State is said to have its own organs of government, natural resources, revenues, laws are made for it, it may go to war, sign international agreements and guarantee rights. Because of this, Justice Kingsmill Moore, in *Comyn v. Attorney General*,[151] decided that the State was a distinct legal person. However, the type or extent of this legal personality has never been determined. As discussed earlier in Part I, as a result of a number of cases, we can say that the State can own property and enter into contracts in its own right,[152] it is capable of enjoying rights[153] and is obliged to protect the rights of its citizens,[154] the State can be sued,[155] and can sue other persons.[156] The relationship between the People and the State was expressed in the case of *Byrne v. Ireland*.[157] Here, Justice Walsh said that 'the State is the creation of the People and is to be governed in accordance with the provisions of the Constitution which was enacted by the People and which can be amended by the People only'. This does not mean that the State is simply an abstract idea however as it is clear that it has a physical application. For example, Article 12.9 states that the President may not leave the State without the consent of the Government. The physical extent of the State is not actually defined in the Constitution. Article 3 refers to the extent of the Irish Free State but the earlier 1922 did not define this entity either. Because of this, it is generally agreed that the State of Ireland is the island of Ireland, minus the area of Northern Ireland, as defined by The Government of Ireland Act, 1920.[158]Article 5 of the Constitution describes Ireland as a 'sovereign, independent, democratic state.'

§2. Local Government

175. While the modern system of Irish local government was created by The Local Government (Ireland) Act 1898, the Constitution originally only indirectly acknowledged this system. Article 12 envisages nominations of presidential candidates by 'Councils of not less than four administrative Counties'. Article 22 also specified than the expressions 'taxation', 'public money', and 'loan' in the definition of a 'Money Bill' do not include monies raised by local authorities for local purposes. Beyond these references, the Constitution did not acknowledge the system of local government.

176. In 1996, The Constitution Review Group, a body set up to examine and recommend changes to the Constitution, recommended express constitutional recognition of the role of local government. This recommendation was supported by the report of the All-Party *Oireachtas* Committee, published in April 1997, which also suggested

150. [1962] IR 216.
151. *Comyn* (n. 19).
152. *Ibid.*
153. *Osheku* (n. 20).
154. *Cox* (n. 21).
155. *Byrne* (n. 14).
156. *Comyn* (n. 19) .
157. *Byrne* (n. 14).
158. Hogan & Whyte (n. 9).

explicit constitutional recognition for local government. Following a referendum in June 1999, Article 28A was inserted into the Constitution. This provision recognizes the role of local government as 'providing a forum for the democratic representation of the local communities, in exercising and performing at a local level powers and function conferred by law …'. This has been described as a 'fairly low level of constitutional protection'.[159] It requires that local authorities be directly elected and that elections must be held every fifth year. The provision also notes that the powers and functions of local authorities are determined by statute.

177. Under the system originally created by the 1898 Act, the local authorities had significant control over aspects such as education, health, roads, etc. Over the years however, responsibility for many of these areas has gradually been reassigned to other bodies.[160] Now the responsibilities of local authorities relate to issues such as housing; planning; environmental protection; provision of recreation and amenities and community infrastructure; etc.

178. Local government is regulated by The Local Government Act 2001, as amended by The Local Government Reform Act 2014, which changed the existing structure. Each local authority is a body corporate, which has perpetual succession, can hold property, sue and be sued. Decision-making power is divided between the elected representatives and the full-time manager who is appointed by the Minister for the Environment, Community and Local Government and is referred to as the 'Chief Executive' since the 2014 Act.

Changes brought in by the 2014 Act included the abolition of all town councils and the merger of some county councils. The reforms came into effect in 2014, to coincide with the local elections of that year.

159. *Ibid.* 486.

160. For example, hospitals, roads, water services, waste collections and third level grants were all under the remit of local county councils but now have either been privatized or have specific public bodies to deal with these issues.

Chapter 2. The State and External Relations

§1. The Role of International Law

179. In Ireland the position in relation to international law is somewhat curious due to the complexities of adding an additional layer of law to a domestically strong constitutional order. Different levels of international law are incorporated differently into the Irish legal system depending on the nature of the laws involved, the ratification process, the general acceptance of the international laws in other jurisdictions and the customs at play. For historic reasons, Ireland's Constitution makes it very clear that only the Irish Parliament can make laws for Ireland, that only the Irish government can make executive decisions on behalf of the People, and that only the Courts established by the Irish Constitution have the right to administer justice in Ireland. The drafters of the 1937 Constitution were keen to assert the independence of the Irish State and to differentiate it from the 1922 Irish Free State which still had some residual British influences. All references and residual powers vested in the Crown were removed and all powers of Westminster to delegate legislation for Ireland were extinguished. In doing so, the 1937 Constitution, perhaps inadvertently, made it slightly more difficult to incorporate international law in Ireland than is the case in many other European jurisdictions.

180. Article 29 of the Irish Constitution entitled 'International Relations' provides the framework for recognizing international law in Ireland, however there are a number of obstacles and challenges provided by the text itself. Article 29.1, for example, prescribes how Ireland 'affirms its devotion to the ideal of peace and friendly co-operation amongst nations founded on international justice and morality' without ever offering any definition as to what is understood by 'international justice and morality'. Article 29.3 is even more problematic. First, in the English language text, this Article provides that 'Ireland accepts the generally recognised principles of international law as its rule of conduct in its relations with other States', which would denote an acceptance by the Irish State of those principles or customs that operate under international law. Tying down the exact definition of these principles has, however, proven to be quite difficult.

An additional complication is the phrase '*ina dtreoir*' which appears in the Irish text (which is the authoritative text in the event of any conflict between the two texts) the translation of which, 'as a guide', does not appear in the English text. In the case of *The State (Sumers Jennings) v. Furlong*,[161] Henchy J stated that the correct position under Irish law is that the general principles of international law are accepted only 'as a guide (*ina dtreoir*) in its relations with other states' and that Article 29.3 should not be seen as tying the hands of the *Oireachtas* when it comes to international law.[162]

161. [1966] IR 183.
162. *Ibid.* 187.

Given that international law principles and rules can only be accepted 'as a guide' in Ireland, a requirement exists for further steps to be taken to give international law the full force of law. Traditionally this process has taken three distinct routes.

181. The first option is for the particular provisions of the international laws in question to be incorporated into the Irish Constitution by way of a constitutional amendment. Such a method has been used in Ireland to give legal force to bodies of international law such as European Union law, international patents law and the International Criminal Court. If such a route is to be undertaken, the people of Ireland must vote to accept the applicability of the particular body of international law to Ireland in a referendum and once the amendment has passed, the *Oireachtas* may then set about implementing the international laws and standards into domestic law. There are varying forms of oversight required by international entities, tribunals and courts. The legal arrangement depends on the type of international law that the State seeks to implement. Such oversight can often be described as either legislative (rule-making), policy based (deciding executive policy), or administrative (administering justice). These are all powers which, as was noted above, are very carefully guarded by the Irish Courts. The passing of a constitutional amendment makes the exercise of these powers by bodies other than the Irish legislature, executive and judiciary constitutionally allowable. This should not be interpreted as a *carte blanche* for the various international bodies concerned to exercise their powers in Ireland. The extent to which their powers can be exercised is still very much limited in scope by the Constitution and the exact manner in which the Constitution provides for the body of international law to have force of law in Ireland. Different bodies of international law have different scope and enjoy the force of law in Ireland to varying degrees.

182. The second manner in which international law is adopted into the Irish legal order is by way of the State simply ratifying the treaty, which technically only requires the signature of the Minister for Foreign Affairs. Article 29.5 declares that every international agreement to which the State becomes a party, except those of a technical and administrative character, must also be laid before the *Dáil*. It further specifies that the State shall not be bound by any international agreement involving a charge upon public funds unless its terms have been approved by the *Dáil*. The practice is that the Government will enter into an international agreement and the agreement will subsequently be laid before the *Dáil*. Therefore, all ratified treaties are laid before the *Dáil*. When international law is ratified without any particular legal intervention it is usually administered in an opt-in manner, where Ireland commits itself to implementing the international law within the jurisdiction without any legal compulsion to do so.

183. Although some attempts have been made to assert rights recognized at international level in domestic courts, the Irish Supreme Court dismissed such arguments in the case of *Re Ó Laighleis* in 1960.[163] In this case, Mr Ó Laighleis sought a declaration

163. [1960] IR 93.

that his internment under The Offences Against the State (Amendment) Act, 1940[164] was contrary to Articles 5 and 6 of the European Convention on Human Rights[165] which guarantee the right to liberty and the right to a fair trial. Ireland had signed and ratified the ECHR Convention but had not incorporated the ECHR Convention into domestic law by that time. Although it should be noted that subsequently in 2003, Ireland did incorporate the ECHR into domestic law. The Supreme Court held that Irish legislation could not be pushed aside merely by virtue of the fact that Ireland had signed up to an international treaty which might conflict with domestic laws, noting that:

> The Court ... cannot accept the idea that the primacy of domestic legislation is displaced by the State becoming a party to the Convention for the Protection of Human Rights and Fundamental Freedoms. Nor can the Court accede to the view that in the domestic forum the Executive is in any way estopped from relying on the domestic law.[166]

Instead of such treaties having full legal effect within the jurisdiction of the signatory State, which the Supreme Court held in *Re Ó Laighléis* is not permissible, most States opt to amend their domestic legislation voluntarily in order to comply with the treaties.

184. Whenever Ireland has been found to be in violation of the ECHR by the Grand Chamber, it has invariably amended its domestic legislation voluntarily, even in cases where the Irish Courts have found no legal reason why the State should be compelled to amend its own domestic law. It should be noted however, that Ireland has tended only to undertake this voluntary action subsequent to adverse findings made against the State, in cases to which Ireland has been a party. This meant that the entire corpus of ECHR law was not voluntarily incorporated into Irish law prior to 2003. The most famous example of such steps having been taken by the Irish State occurred in the *Norris v. Attorney General*[167] and *Norris v. Ireland*[168] series of cases. Norris challenged the constitutionality of a nineteenth century legislative provision, which criminalized certain sexual acts only between males without criminalizing similar sexual conduct between females. Having been unsuccessful before the Irish Courts, he subsequently took his case to the European Court for Human Rights and was successful in having the offending legislation declared incompatible with Article 8 of the ECHR which guarantees the right to privacy. As a result of this judgment from the ECtHR, Ireland subsequently decriminalized homosexual acts with the enacting of The Criminal Law (Sexual Offences) Act, 1993. There was no constitutional or other legal imperative under which Ireland had to act to give effect to the judgment of the

164. This Act was initially introduced as an emergency measure used to intern members of the IRA without trial who it was felt would threaten Irish neutrality during World War Two by launching attacks on the United Kingdom. The same powers were subsequently used by the Irish State during further IRA campaigns and ultimately the tactic was replicated by the British Government as a method to deal with the Provisional IRA in the late 1970s and 1980s.
165. Hereinafter referred to as 'ECHR'.
166. [1960] IR 93 125.
167. *Norris* (n. 32).
168. [1988] 13 EHRR 186.

European Court of Human Rights. However, as a contracting State, Ireland opted into wilfully amending its domestic legislation to reflect the judgments of the Court. Should a State which is a party to the ECHR fail to reflect a judgment of the Court in their domestic legislation the option of monetary fines and ultimate expulsion from the ECHR Convention is available to the Court.

185. The final manner in which international law can be incorporated into Irish law and the Irish legal order is by the way of domestic Irish legislation. Article 29.6 of the Constitution makes it clear that no international treaty will form part of the domestic law of Ireland unless it is provided for by the *Oireachtas*. As Byrne and McCutcheon note:

> most treaties to which Ireland becomes a party to are never incorporated because they relate solely to the state's rights and duties with respect to other States or, in the case of human rights treaties, because the rights they confer are already protected in Irish law. Where incorporation takes places, it is, for most part, achieved indirectly: the Oireachtas gives carefully defined effect to the treaty by mirroring the most important of its provisions in the body of an Act[169]

The vast majority of these treaties tend to be of a technical nature because they govern the relationship between States and the regulation of disputes arising therefrom. Usually, most of the treaties to which Ireland is a party are not justiciable in Irish Courts because the very nature of the treaties precludes any need to incorporate them into domestic law. A number of particularly important international law treaties have been transposed into domestic law; the most prominent example being the ECHR which was enacted into Irish Law through The ECHR Act, 2003.

186. When Ireland ratifies a treaty either by merely signing it or transposing it into domestic legislation there still exists a proviso that the legislation, or the effect of the obligations placed upon Ireland by virtue of ratifying the treaty, must always pass the test of constitutionality. Only those treaties which have been incorporated into Irish law *via* the Constitution can enjoy the protection of certainty as to their legality, although treaties incorporated by legislation enjoy a presumption, albeit a rebuttable one, as to their constitutionality.

§2. The International Criminal Court

187. When the International Criminal Court was established in 1998, the Irish government signalled that they wished to ratify the Rome Statute, which brought the Court into existence. In order to do so, Ireland would have to submit to the jurisdiction of the International Criminal Court in certain criminal matters (predominantly war crimes and crimes against humanity). Given that the Irish Constitution asserts Irish sovereignty and the right to try offenders,[170] submission to the jurisdiction of the International Criminal Court required the passing of a constitutional amendment to

169. Raymond Byrne and Paul McCutcheon, *Byrne and McCutcheon on the Irish Legal System* (5th edn, Bloomsbury 2009) 795.

170. Articles 5 and 38.

legitimize the partial transfer of the sovereign powers of the State in this limited criminal law sphere. On 27 March 2002, the Irish people voted overwhelmingly in favour of the Twenty-Third Amendment of the Constitution which inserted Article 29.9 into the Irish Constitution.[171] In doing so, the people of Ireland accepted the limited role of the International Criminal Court as established by the Rome Statute, however it should be noted that no powers beyond those which are contained in the Rome Statute can be constitutionally transferred to the International Criminal Court.

§3. The European Union

188. Since 1972, when Ireland first joined the European Union, Ireland has incorporated the body of international law known as EU law into the Irish Constitution in a manner which has a very wide scope. On 8 June 1972, the Irish people passed the Third Amendment to the Constitution, which allowed Ireland to become a member of the (then) European Community by giving the Government the right to ratify the various treaties which formed the body of European Community Law. A clause was added to what is now Article 29.4.10°, which states in that:

> No provision of this Constitution invalidates laws enacted, acts done or measures adopted by the State which are necessitated by the obligations of membership of the European Union or of the Communities, or prevents laws enacted, acts done or measures adopted by the European Union or by the Communities or by institutions thereof, or by bodies competent under the Treaties establishing the Communities, from having the force of law in the State.

Essentially, the wording of this provision means that any provision of the Irish Constitution which would normally render a provision of EU law unconstitutional cannot do so as long as the EU law or rule was one which was necessitated by the treaties establishing what we now know as EU law. The body of EU law was incorporated into Irish law in such a manner because EU law demands that it should enjoy supremacy over all national laws (including national constitutions) in areas where the various treaties give the EU competence. As Tomkin notes: 'Article 29.4.10° ensures that Ireland could fully comply with its obligations under EC law, without fear of breaching the Constitution.'[172] While it is accepted that EU law enjoys a great scope of incorporation into national law this incorporation is limited to the scope contained within the various treaties which make up the body of laws known as EU law; EU law has no scope and does not enjoy any force of law or constitutional protection in spheres outside the ambit of the treaties. EU law has become extremely dynamic and expansive in recent years. In the years since 1987, the various competencies and scope of EU law have been altered on no less than seven occasions, with new treaties requiring ratification on each occasion by each Member State. Ireland, rather uniquely in Europe, requires

171. Article 29.9 reads; 'The State may ratify the Rome Statute of the International Criminal Court done at Rome on the 17th day of July, 1998.'

172. Jonothan Tomkin, 'Implementing Community Legislation into National Law' (2004) Judicial Studies Institute Journal Volume 4 No. 2 130 132.

a referendum on each occasion as a result of the decision of the Irish Courts in the case of *Crotty v. An Taoiseach.*[173] Here the Supreme Court held that each time the competencies of the EU change from treaty to treaty, the Irish government must seek a new mandate from the Irish people by way of constitutional amendment to further authorize the new transfer of powers and sovereignty from the Irish State to the EU. Thus, EU law, as a body of international law in Ireland enjoys a large ambit and is very strongly incorporated into Irish law but only to the extent to which the Irish people have acceded in the various referendums.

§4. Extra-territoriality

189. The Nineteenth Amendment to the Constitution, which gave a constitutional footing to the Belfast Agreement,[174] also introduced Article 29.8, which provides that: 'The State may exercise extra-territorial jurisdiction in accordance with the generally recognised principles of international law.' This matter had previously come up for consideration in the case *Re Article 26 and the Criminal Law (Jurisdiction) Bill 1975.*[175] The case turned on the former Article 3, which, before it was amended, stated: 'Pending the re-integration of the national territory, and without prejudice to the right of the parliament and government established by this constitution to exercise jurisdiction over the whole territory, the laws enacted by the parliament shall have the like area and extent of application as the laws of *Saorstát Éireann* and the like extra-territorial effect'. The Court had to consider whether the former Parliament of *Saorstát Éireann*[176] had the power to legislate with extra-territorial effect and it concluded that it did, pointing to the dictum of Chief Justice O'Higgins in the *Lotus* case:

> It is established in international law by the decision of the Permanent Court of International Justice in the Lotus Case that every sovereign State has power to legislate with extra-territorial effect in the sense that it may enact that acts or omissions done outside its borders are criminal offences which may be successfully prosecuted within its borders – this is sometimes called the jurisdiction to prescribe – provided that the events, acts or persons to which its enactment applies bear upon the peace, order and good government of the legislating State.[177]

The insertion of Article 29.8 put this on a firmer footing and as Hogan and Whyte have noted:

173. *Crotty* (n. 16).
174. The Belfast or 'Good Friday' Agreement of 1998 was a major political agreement which set out the current relationship of the Republic of Ireland, Northern Ireland and the United Kingdom. It also involved the decommissioning of weapons held by paramilitary groups and the normalization of security arrangements in Northern Ireland.
175. [1977] IR 129.
176. The Free State of Ireland – the name designated to the State in 1921.
177. (1927) PCIJ Ser A, No 10.

> [By] breaking the connection between this jurisdiction and the powers of the Parliament of Saorstát Éireann, it ensures that the power of the Oireachtas to legislate with extra-territorial effect is not defined by reference to the equivalent power of the older Parliament but may develop organically in line with modern public international law.[178]

The new Article 3.1, which replaced the former provision, provides that the laws enacted by the *Oireachtas* 'shall have the same area and extent of application as the laws enacted by the Parliament that existed immediately before the coming into operation of this Constitution'.

178. Hogan & Whyte (n. 9) 562.

Part IV. Citizenship and the Administration of Justice

Chapter 1. Rules Concerning Nationality and Relevance of Nationality

§1. General

190. Prior to 1 January 2005, in a manner similar to the United States, every person born on the island of Ireland was automatically entitled to Irish citizenship. This was initially regulated by The Irish Nationality and Citizenship Acts 1935 and 1937. These were repealed and replaced in 1956 and later amended a number of times, the most recent being in 2004. Prior to 2004, it was believed that the amendment of the old Articles 2 and 3 of the Constitution, as part of the Good Friday Agreement in 1999 reinforced the right of citizenship by birth. However, a referendum in June 2004 and the subsequent passing of The Irish Nationality and Citizenship Act, 2004 significantly altered this position and restricted the automatic right to citizenship The referendum amended Article 9.2 to provide that citizenship would only be guaranteed to those born on the island of Ireland who, at the time of their birth, have one parent who is or is entitled to become an Irish citizen. It also provided for further change by legislation and the 2004 Act moderately expanded the grounds for claiming citizenship. Irish citizenship can now be acquired by birth (subject to at least one parent also being an Irish citizen or being entitled to Irish citizenship), decent, marriage or through naturalization in accordance with the law. Legislation also provides for dual and multiple nationality. Many people born in Northern Ireland are British as well as being Irish citizens.

Chapter 2. Fundamental Rights and Liberties

§1. The Structural Basis of Constitutional Protection of Individual Rights

I. Introduction

191. Articles 40 to 44 of the Constitution carry the title 'Fundamental Rights' and are generally seen as the main source of constitutional rights under the Irish Constitution. The rights contained therein have been central to the development of what essentially amounts to an Irish Bill of Rights. These provisions have been the basis for many far reaching decisions of the Irish Courts and the further development of rights discourse. However, it is important to note that Articles 40 to 44 are not the sole source of Irish Constitutional rights and many other provisions of the Constitution have been successfully invoked to ground and assert rights.[179]

The language and tone of the provisions regarding fundamental rights in the Irish Constitution is very much rooted in the natural law tradition, with rights typically described in language such as 'inalienable' and 'imprescriptible'. Although there is a strong Roman Catholic influence throughout the Irish Constitution, natural law in the context of the Constitution does not mean an exclusive focus on Roman Catholic doctrine and in some instances decisions rooted in natural law have been expressly contrary to Roman Catholic teachings.[180]

II. Who Is a Citizen and Who Is Entitled to the Protection of Rights

192. Although the Irish Constitution consistently uses the expression citizen when referring to who can enjoy the protection of certain rights under the Constitution including the equality guarantee, the freedom of expression and the freedom of assembly. This has long been broadly interpreted to mean any person can avail of such rights rather than it being the sole preserve of Irish citizens. Other rights, such as the rights of families, are not expressly noted as rights of citizens. Thus the Courts have, on many occasions, noted that personal rights, rooted as they are in natural law, apply to every person who seeks to assert them and are not just the preserve of Irish citizens.[181] Although it is not absolutely clear whether non-citizens can invoke the other rights in the Constitution outside of Articles 40–44, or whether they can challenge the constitutional validity of legislation, there is a general acceptance that such avenues are available to

179. *See* Hogan & Whyte (n. 9) 386.

180. *See for example* the decision in McGee (n. 32) a case which concerned the use of contraceptives.

181. *See for example*, the case of *Finn v. Attorney General* [1983] IR 154, 159 where Barrington J noted that 'the Constitution accepts that those rights derive not from the law but from the nature of man and society, and guarantees to protect them accordingly.'

non-citizens. The situation for non-human entities and legal persons is a little less clear. Although the Courts initially suggested that non-human persons could not avail of the constitutional rights which were intended to protect citizens[182] the Courts are now willing to accept that shareholders in non-human entities can enjoy the constitutional rights that are connected with such entities.[183] The Court however moved on from this position in *Iarnród Éireann v. Ireland*[184] when the Court recognized that certain rights, with a particular focus on the rights that are connected to property, must be available to non-human persons and cannot be too narrowly defined in these cases.

III. The Balancing of Constitutional Rights

193. Very often when it comes to constitutional rights, the assertion of a right by one person or group will put them at odds with another. Irish law for example protects the right to bodily integrity of individuals but the rights of society on public health grounds can often conflict with this. In order to deal with such situations the Courts in Ireland have tended to carefully weigh the rights of all parties and either come to some form of balance whereby both rights can be accommodated or, more typically, the Courts tend to invoke a hierarchy of rights and subsume one under the other.[185] In the event that the legislature has already attempted some form of balancing act of the competing claims of various rights through legislation, the Courts have laid down a clear test which they are to follow in order to assess if the balance proposed by the legislature is an appropriate one.[186] The Court is obliged not to impose their view of whether the balance struck is correct or desirable but rather to 'determine from an objective stance whether the balance contained in the impugned legislation is so contrary to reason and fairness as to constitute an unjust attack on some individual's constitutional rights'.[187] This is not to say however that a Court cannot overrule an attempted balancing of rights by the legislature. As the Courts are often willing and able to strike law down when the need arises.

IV. The Limiting of Rights

194. No constitutional right under the Irish Constitution can be considered absolute. As seen above, in some circumstances a balance between competing rights must be achieved. Constitutional rights are often subject to limitations and restrictions due to competing rights or the needs of society as a whole. The Constitution achieves this in a number of ways; most rights are expressly qualified in one form or another. Many personal rights can only be vindicated 'as far as practicable'; the Right to life of the unborn is put on an equal footing with the right to life of the mother and the

182. *See for example*, *Quinn's Supermarket Ltd. v. Attorney General* (n. 76).
183. *PMPS Ltd. & Others v. Attorney General* [1983] IR 339.
184. [1996] 3IR 32 1.
185. *See* para. 57.
186. *Tuohy v. Courtney* [1994] 3IR.
187. *Ibid.* 47.

right of freedom of expression is subject to qualifications such as the need to respect public order and morality. For example, in the case of *Murray v. Ireland*[188] although the Supreme Court recognized that a married couple did indeed have a constitutional right to procreate and start a family, it was held that it was entirely legitimate for the State in this instance to restrict this right due to the particular circumstances of the case. This decision was reached mainly due to the fact that the couple in question were being incarcerated at the behest of the State after having been found guilty of capital murder.

195. The limiting of constitutional rights is, of course, a jurisdiction which has to be exercised with extreme caution. Over time, the Courts have adopted a proportionality test in order to ensure that any limiting of constitutional rights is only done with a view to achieving as little limitation of constitutional rights as possible. The greater the interference and limitation of constitutional rights is, the greater the need for the State to demonstrate the importance of the objective they seek to obtain. In *Heaney v. Ireland*,[189] the Court outlined the extent of the proportionality test to be applied in cases concerning the restriction and limitation of rights. Firstly, the limitation of rights must be rationally connected to the objective of said limitation. Secondly, the restrictions must not be arbitrary, unfair or based on irrational considerations. Third, the extent to which the right is limited or impaired must be as little as possible. Finally, the actual effects on the right which has been interfered with must be proportionate with the objective sought. In *Ryan v. Ireland*,[190] the Court accepted that Mrs Ryan had a constitutional right to bodily integrity and that by adding fluoride to the drinking-water supply, the State was interfering with that right. The Court went on to rule however that the adding of fluoride to the drinking-water supply was a legitimate limitation of Mrs Ryan's rights on the grounds of the common good and the consequent public health benefits that are typically associated with the improvements to dental health that result from fluoride exposure.

V. Enumerated and 'Unenumerated' Rights

196. Personal fundamental rights in the Irish Constitution have tended to be subdivided into two distinct categories: enumerated rights, which are expressly mentioned in the constitutional text and unenumerated rights, which have developed over time as the increasingly active judiciary has 'recognized' them. Enumerated Rights are discussed in further detail below. Unenumerated rights are essentially rights which are not specifically written into the Constitution. They have developed in Ireland as a result of a judiciary willing to embrace activism and owe much to the specific wording of Article 40.3.2° which prescribes that '[t]he State shall *in particular*, by its law protect as best it may from unjust attack ... the life, person good name, and property rights of every citizen'.[191] The inference taken from this provision by the Courts has been that since certain rights are to be protected 'in particular' it logically follows that

188. *Murray* (n. 54).
189. [1994] 3IR 593.
190. *Ryan* (n. 45).
191. Emphasis added.

other rights must exist in order for the rights prescribed in Article 40.3.2 to be given special attention within the hierarchy of rights. Some have drawn parallels between this development and the Ninth Amendment provision in the US Constitutional Bill of Rights.[192] However, the Irish constitutional position is perhaps not a comparable example. There are suggestions that the Irish experience is more unique and owes more to judicial activism than constitutional design.[193]

197. There is no one agreed source of 'unenumerated rights', in fact a number of differing justifications have been used throughout the case law. In Ireland, like in the United States, natural law has been offered as one such source[194] although the language used occasionally hints at a more Christian focused understanding of natural law than in the United States, whereby the 'Christian and democratic nature of the state' has been used to recognize certain 'unenumerated rights' in the Courts;[195] language more in line with human rights discourse has been used to justify the recognition of rights under a doctrine whereby rights are seen as inherently vested in citizens by virtue of their human personality.[196] Other constitutional provisions are often used as the inspiration for the recognition of 'unenumerated rights',[197] including, somewhat controversially, Article 45[198] which, under its own terms, is itself not expressly justiciable by the Courts. In rarer circumstances, certain rights which have been traditionally recognized as rights under the Common Law have found their way into constitutional rights discourse via the 'unenumerated rights' doctrine.[199]

198. The doctrine was first fully and formally recognized in the case of *Ryan v. Attorney General*[200] in 1963, where the Plaintiff who was opposed to the fluoridation of drinking water sought to assert an unenumerated constitutional right to bodily integrity in order to have the enabling statue declared unconstitutional., Although Mrs Ryan did succeed in having her right to bodily integrity recognized, she was ultimately unsuccessful in her own action based on the particular facts of the case. The court held that such a right was secondary to the common good and health benefits that could be obtained by the fluoridation of drinking water. Kenny J in the High Court, with the Supreme Court later agreeing, held that the rights protected by the Irish Constitution included the enumerated rights prescribed in the constitutional text '*and* other personal rights of the citizen which have to be formulated and devised by the High Court.'[201] Even in this very first instance, perhaps in an attempt to pre-empting some of the criticism which would later be directed toward the doctrine, Kenny J did sound a note of caution to his fellow members of the judiciary in his noting that the power of the Courts to recognize such rights was 'a jurisdiction to be exercised with caution'.

192. *See generally* Forde & Leonard (n. 18) 297.
193. *See generally* David Gwynn Morgan, *A Judgment too far? Judicial activism and the Constitution* (Cork University Press 2001).
194. *McGee* (n. 32) and *Murray* (n. 54).
195. *Ryan* (n. 45) and *Fawley* (n. 48).
196. *Paperlink* (n. 50) and *McGee* (n. 32).
197. Art 8 *Ó Beoláin* [2001] 2 IR 279; Art 34 *Macauley* (n. 58); Art 38 *State (Healy) v. Donoghue* [1976] IR 325; Art 41 *McGee* (n. 33).
198. *Murtagh Properties v. Cleary* [1972] IR 330.
199. *Garvey v. Ireland* [1981] IR 75.
200. *Ryan* (n. 45).
201. *Ibid.* 311.

199. The newly arrived doctrine was given a more solid footing in *McGee v. Attorney General*[202] when the full extent of its power and potential was recognized. The Plaintiff, a married woman who already had given birth to a number of children was advised that there was a serious risk to her life if she were to become pregnant again. Contraceptives were prohibited however in Ireland by The Custom Consolidation Act 1876 which, although a pre-independence enactment, remained in force and had subsequently been amended in by The Criminal Law (Amendment) Act 1935. The Plaintiff sought to assert an unenumerated constitutional right and accordingly to have the offending section of the amended 1876 Act deemed unconstitutional, on the basis that it unjustly infringed her unenumerated right. Although she was initially unsuccessful in the High Court, the Supreme Court did rule in her favour, holding that by virtue of natural law and the rights which inhered in Mrs McGee as a human person, which meant that she did in fact enjoy a constitutionally protected right to martial privacy. The Court went on to hold that the 1876 Act, as amended, never survived the enactment of the 1937 Constitution and, consequently, deemed the *de facto* ban on contraceptives to be unconstitutional and void *ab initio*.

200. While by their very nature, a definitive list of unenumerated rights which could be recognized cannot be offered, the main rights recognized by the Courts to date under the doctrine are listed below:

The right to disassociate was recognized in Education Company v. Fitzpatrick No 2[203] where a picket which sought to force an employer to only employ unionized staff was held to be an infringement on the rights of employees who did not wish to join a union.

The right to bodily integrity was recognized in the Ryan[204] fluoridation case and later emphasized in McGee[205] which concerned marital privacy vis a vis contraceptives and also in Re a Ward of Court[206] which centred around the right to remove medical intervention for a patient in a persistent vegetative state.

The right to marry was mentioned obiter in Ryan[207] and subsequent cases such as Murray[208] and Norris.[209] The right is now expressly recognized by the thirty-fourth amendment, passed in 2015, which enshrined the right to marry for all

202. *McGee* (n. 32).
203. [1961] IR 345.
204. *Ryan* (n. 45).
205. *McGee* (n. 32).
206. *Re a Ward of Court* (n. 206).
207. *Ryan* (n. 45).
208. *Murray* (n. 54).
209. *Norris* (n. 32).

heterosexual and same-sex couples, albeit with certain restrictions around the age and relationships between the parties that are seeking to marry.[210]

The right to earn a livelihood was recognized in Murtagh Properties v. Cleary[211] where the picketing of premises on the basis of the employment of non-union staff was held to be unconstitutional. This is not to say that one is entitled to do any job and that the State cannot legitimately limit entry into certain professions by imposing qualification or language requirements.[212]

The right of access to the Courts was acknowledged in Macauley v. Minister for Posts and Telegraphs,[213] where a requirement to get the permission of the Attorney General before initiating an action against a Minister was considered an unconstitutional interference. There is some debate however as to why this is considered an unenumerated right rather than merely a logical follow-on from Article 34.3.1 which establishes the jurisdiction of the Courts.[214]

The right to marital privacy was recognized in McGee[215] whereby the legislative prohibition on contraceptives was held by the Supreme Court to be an unlawful interference with the privacy of a married couple.

The right to procreate was recognized in McGee[216] and later in Murray.[217] However, in the latter case the Court held that legitimate restrictions could be placed upon the right in certain circumstances.

The general right to privacy was recognized in Norris v. Attorney General[218] and Kennedy v. Ireland.[219] The right was not deemed sufficient in Norris to declare the criminal prohibition of homosexual relations between consenting males unconstitutional. The Court held that such a prohibition was justified on grounds of maintaining public morality with special reference being made to the Christian

210. *See O'Shea and O'Shea v. Ireland* and the Attorney General (Unreported, High Court, 17 Oct. 2006, Laffoy J.) for exploration of legality on relationship restrictions to marriage.
211. *Murtagh Properties v. Cleary* (n. 198).
212. *See Kenny v. Dental Council* [2009] 4 IR 321 (qualification requirements) and *Groener v. Minister for Education [1989] ECR 3967* (Irish language requirements).
213. *Macauley* (n. 58).
214. *See* Hogan & Whyte (n. 9).
215. *McGee* (n. 32).
216. *Ibid.*
217. *Murray* (n. 54).
218. *Norris* (n. 32).
219. Kennedy (n. 53) – this case concerned the bugging of journalists' telephones. However not all instances of surveillance are unconstitutional.

teachings contained in the preamble to the Constitution.[220] In Re a Ward of Court (No. 2)[221] the right to privacy was held to include a right to refuse medical treatment, even if the refusal was to have fatal consequences.

The right to communicate was recognized in Attorney General v. Paperlink Ltd[222] in a case which concerned the legality of the State's monopoly on post services. The Court held that the very act of communication was held to be such a fundamental aspect of humanity that such an unenumerated right had to be acknowledged.

The right to travel within Ireland was acknowledged initially, albeit obiter, in the Ryan case[223]. The right to travel outside of the State requires a passport which was confirmed in the case of State (M) v. Attorney General.[224] Here the parents of a child who wished to bring their daughter abroad with them successfully challenged the State's decision not to issue the child a passport.

The right to legal counsel: although the right to have legal counsel provided for on criminal charges has been long recognized in both domestic law and under the terms of the ECHR[225] this right was also recognized as having a constitutional basis in State (Healy) v. Donoghue.[226] This right has also been recognized as extending to certain non-criminal spheres. In the case of inquiries and State investigations, where the constitutionally protected right to a good name of a citizen is in issue the Courts have held that the right to legal counsel exists. This right has gradually been extended to cover family law proceedings and the fair administration of free civil legal aid.[227]

The right to know the identity of one's natural mother was acknowledged in I.O'T v. B[228] where the Applicants' were informally adopted. The Court held that adoption led to certain expectations as to information with regards one's identity. The Court did note however that this right would however have to be administered

220. *See* a discussion of *Norris* (n. 32) 88.
221. *Re a Ward of Court* (No. 2) (n. 206).
222. *Paperlink* (n. 50).
223. *Ryan* (n. 45).
224. [1979] IR 73.
225. *See* Criminal Justice (Legal Aid) Act, 1962 and Art 6(3)(c) of the ECHR.
226. [1976] 1 IR 325.
227. Although there is no clear authority that all Plaintiffs are entitled to free civil legal aid the Courts have expressed opinions which suggest that such free legal aid schemes(which are legislative in nature) must in fact adhere to certain set standards in order to vindicate the unenumerated constitutional rights of the litigants involved in a civil suit.
228. [1998] 2 IR 321.

on a case-by-case basis, as there is often a conflict of rights between the adopted child's right to information and the natural mother's right to privacy.[229]

The right to fair procedures in decision-making has been recognized by the Courts as an embodiment of natural justice. A similar right could be said to exist under the Common Law as the right has gained a constitutional footing through the Supreme Court case of Garvey v. Ireland.[230] A decision which centred on whether the Government of the day had the power to remove the then most senior sitting Garda (police officer) in the State from office.

201. Although it cannot be definitively stated whether the doctrine of unenumerated rights has run its course, it would certainly appear that the enthusiasm with which the Irish Courts had greeted the doctrine, in particular in the 1970s and 1980s, has certainly diminished – the most recent example being the finding that no unenumerated right to clean swimming water exists in *Duffy v. Clare County Council & Ors.*[231] Whilst the doctrine clearly has certain benefits, particularly with regards the recognition of fundamental rights which are not expressly recognized in the written text of the Constitution, its inherent ambiguity inevitably leads to significant uncertainty as to the limits of rights discourse in Ireland.[232]

202. Critics of unenumerated rights maintain that recognizing so many rights not expressly contained within the text of the Constitution or prescribed by statute, allows the judiciary to effectively infringe upon the exclusive law-making power of the legislature and therefore undermine the strict separation of powers that is contained within the Irish Constitution. The counter-argument holds that the doctrine allows for a great deal of flexibility and permits the Constitution to develop as a living document which changes over time. When considering the future of the doctrine, the Constitutional Review Group, an expert group established to consider constitutional reform, suggested in 1996 that 'there does not appear to be any objective method of ascertaining what these personal rights are'[233] but they did however note the beneficial nature of the doctrine. The 1996 Report from the Group went on to conclude that the doctrine of unenumerated rights should ultimately be eliminated by amending the Constitution to expressly recognize the fundamental rights that have been already recognized with some scope for incorporation of international human rights norms.[234]

229. *Ibid.* 349.
230. [1981] IR 75.
231. [2013] IEHC 51.
232. Most scholars note that many of the rights could justifiably be recognized under other provisions of the Constitution.
233. The Constitutional Review Group, *Report of the Constitution Review Group*, (Stationery Office, 1996) 189.
234. *Ibid.* 235.

§2. Personal Rights

I. Equality before the Law

A. Introduction

203. The equality guarantee in the Irish Constitution is the very first enumerated personal right expressed within the text of the Fundamental Rights section (Articles 40-44) of the Irish Constitution. The guarantee itself is contained within 40.1 and is presented in two clauses. First, the text notes that all [people][235] should be held equal before the law. The second clause brings an Aristotelian understanding of equality to mind with the proviso noting that the State can have due regard in its enactments for differences of 'capacity, physical and moral, and of social function'. As Walsh J noted in what is now his famous pronouncement on gender equality: 'Article 40 does not require identical treatment of all persons without recognition of differences in relevant circumstances but it forbids arbitrary discrimination. It imports the Aristotelian concept that justice demands that we treat equals equally and unequals unequally.[236]

204. Article 40.1, like many of the rights under the Irish Constitution, is directly addressed to the State. The Courts have hinted at a broader ambit for Article 40.1 in *The State (Lynch) v. Cooney*[237] when the Courts examined the impact of the equality provision on the reviewability of a ministerial decision regarding broadcasting. Article 40.1 has also had an impact on Common Law rules and doctrines. In *W. v. W.*[238] a Common Law rule that a wife's domicile was that of her husband's was struck down as putting married women in an unequal position with both their husbands and single women. The scope of Article 40.1 is not merely limited to legislation but also encompasses the manner in which legislative rules and regulations are administered and interpreted by both the executive and the Courts themselves. In *East Donegal Co-op Ltd. v. Attorney General*[239] a provision of an agricultural Act effectively allowed a Government Minister to set aside legislation for 'any particular business' if he so wished. The Minster could effectively pick and choose who would be subject to the law. The Court held that to do so would be an infringement on the equality guarantee. A crucial factor for the Court in this instance was the fact that the legislation itself lacked a justification measure. In *The People (Attorney General) v. O'Driscoll*[240] the Court said that it would have no hesitation in invoking Article 40.1 to overturn a prior ruling if it could be shown that the Court discriminated against two defendants on ethnic grounds.

---

235. The text uses the wording citizen but *see* para. 192 above for discussion on this.
236. *De Búrca v. Attorney General* [1976] IR 38 68.
237. [1982] IR 337.
238. [1993] 2 IR 476. *See also The State (D.P.P.) v. Walsh* [1981] IR 412 where the Common Law defence of martial coercion was struck down as an unjust infringement against Article 40.1.
239. [1970] IR 317.
240. (1972) 1 Frewen 351.

B. Application of 40.1 by the Courts

205. The Irish Courts have had what could be best described as a somewhat ambivalent attitude towards applying the provisions of Article 40.1, which stands in marked contrast to the Court's open and willing engagement with the unenumerated rights doctrine. A very similar clause in the Fourteenth Amendment to the US Constitution has generated a huge volume of often controversial jurisprudence; however the equality provision has never quite captured the judicial imagination in the Irish context. In fact, it has long been noted that the Irish Courts have actually given 40.1 an unusually wide berth and have often gone very much out of their way to actually avoid actively engaging with its terms.[241]

When faced with Applicants seeking to rely upon Article 40.1, the Courts have tended to ask whether particular legal discriminations were permissible under Article 40.1. *In Dillane v. Attorney General,*[242] when a law which granted immunity for serving police officers for certain legal actions was challenged, the Court focused on whether the discrimination in favour of police officers was justifiable on grounds of reasonableness. In the circumstances and given the role played by the police in society, it was held reasonable that such an immunity be offered to them and thus was held not to infringe the equality guarantee within Article 40.1.

206. The Court further elaborated on this general point in *O'B. v. S.*[243] when assessing whether a piece of legislation was discriminatory in light of Article 40.1. It was held that the object and nature of the legislation must be assessed. Furthermore, any discrimination must be relevant to the aims of the legislation in question and must not be arbitrary, unreasonable or unjust.

Direct applications of 40.1 by the Courts are rare and are often avoided by the Courts where possible in favour of invoking a different Article of the Constitution. Gender discrimination cases have however given rise to a number of successful applications. In *De Búrca v. Attorney General*[244] a section in The Juries Act 1927 which amounted to an effective ban on female jury participation for the majority of the population was held to infringe the equality guarantee. In *TO'G v. Attorney General*[245] adoption rules which permitted widows to adopt children without arbitrary pre-conditions but required widowers to have children already under their care in order to be eligible for this technical exemption was struck down as unconstitutionally discriminatory.[246]

207. Outside of the gender equality sphere there have been a limited number of successful applications based in part on Article 40.1. Issues concerning elections and referendums have been partially at least partially decided on the basis of the equality guarantee where interference in the democratic process has been established.[247]

241. *See generally* Casey (n. 84).
242. [1980] ILRM 167.
243. [1984] IR 316.
244. *De Búrca* (n. 236).
245. [1985] ILRM 61.
246. *See also* the cases of *McKinley v. Minister for Defence* and *SM v. Ireland* [2007] IEHC 280 which both concerned gender discrimination.
247. *See McKenna v. An Taoiseach (No. 2)* (n. 38).

In the case of *An Blascaod Mór Teoranta v. Commissioners of Public Works*[248] however the Court acknowledged that a technical exemption in compulsory purchase legislation which only applied to descendants of people born on a particular island was unconstitutionally discriminatory.[249]

C. *Refusal by the Courts to invoke Article 40.1*

208. The Irish Courts have, at times, appeared to have taken very deliberate steps to avoid invoking the equality guarantee. At times the Courts have: accepted that an alleged discrimination was justified, decided a case on the basis of a different constitutional provision (often when a direct application of Article 40.1 would appear to be the more straightforward solution) and have even occasionally flat out refused to acknowledge that any discrimination took place at all. Casey notes that,[250] the Courts 'have given it a restricted ambit; they prefer to decide cases on other grounds; and they have often justified statutory discriminations by reasoning that does not probe very deeply'.

209. The Courts have tended towards a very strict interpretation of the qualifications in the text of the Article 40.1 equality guarantee. One such qualification which the Courts have often relied upon is the requirement that in order to establish that any unconstitutional discrimination has taken place, an Applicant must prove that such discrimination was based upon aspects of human personality. Thus, in *Quinns Supermarket Ltd. v. Attorney General*[251] discrimination on religious grounds was alleged and the fact that the Applicant was a legal entity as opposed to a human person excluded the Applicant from the protection of the equality guarantee, which the Court held was directed at human persons by virtue of their innate humanity. In *Madigan v. Attorney General*[252] the Applicant sought to avail of the protection of the equality guarantee by alleging that he was being discriminated against as a property owner due to the levying of a new property tax. The Court held that the owning of property was not an inherent facet of human personhood and accordingly refused to invoke Article 40.1.

210. Classifications of citizens and groups of citizens into groups and sub groups has long been accepted and justified. By way of example, the Constitution itself sets a number of different age limits for different activities and recognizes the different roles played by different genders, languages, members of constitutional offices etc. Accordingly, such discriminations, which in some cases could be claimed to be prima facie infringements of the equality guarantee, are allowed so long as there is no further arbitrary discrimination within the outlined classifications. The Courts have tended to hypothesize as to the rationality of such classifications by the legislature when assessing whether a legislative based segregation into certain distinct classes should be constitutionally permissible under Article 40.1.

248. [2000] 1 ILRM 401.
249. *See also McMahon v. Leahy* [1984] IR 525 where a policy decision to treat one on the run political prisoner differently to others was held to be discriminatory.
250. Casey (n. 84) 451.
251. [1972] IR 1.
252. [1986] ILRM 136.

211. In The *People (DPP) v. Quilligan and O'Reilly (No. 3)*[253] the different treatment of suspects arrested under anti-terrorism legislation compared with those arrested on suspicion of other offences was upheld by the Courts as a justified classification. In *Somjee v. Minister for Justice*[254] differing rules for married male and female applicants for naturalization where upheld by the Court. The Court held that the different and preferential treatment given to female applicants, was not a discrimination against married male applicants, but was in fact a privilege conferred upon married woman for various social, economic and political reasons which exist in the jurisdiction from which the female applicant arrived.[255]

In *The State (Hartley) v. Governor of Mountjoy Prison*[256] the Court upheld the constitutionality of a situation whereby alternate extradition arrangements were made for differing jurisdictions. The key requirement here was that all of the suspects being extradited to the same jurisdiction were being treated equally which enabled the different treatment between jurisdictions to be permissible. This decision has attracted criticism as it is contended that it allowed the scope of classification to be set too broadly[257]. In *Norris v. Attorney General,*[258] a case which attracted significant criticism,[259] the Court upheld a nineteenth century legislative provision which criminalized certain sexual acts between males only with no corresponding criminalization of similar sexual conduct between females. The Court reasoned that such a classification was in fact permissible because 'gross indecency between males ... require[ing]s prohibition [due to] the social problem which it creates, while ... sexual conduct between females [is] not only [quantitatively] different but [also poses] no such social problem[s].'[260]

212. Not all classification of citizens by the legislature can be deemed to be beyond the scope of Article 40.1. In *De Búrca v. Attorney General*[261] a classification in legislation which effectively confined the right to serve on a jury almost exclusively to men was held unconstitutional and was considered to be an over-inclusive classification. The Courts have also found that certain classifications have been under-inclusive to such a degree that they infringe the equality guarantee enshrined in Article 40.1. In *Dennehy v. Minister for Social Welfare*[262] the restriction of certain social welfare benefits which only benefitted female spouses was held to be both arbitrary and discriminatory, although it should be noted that the distinction between male and female spouses was upheld on other grounds.

213. Other constitutional provisions are very often invoked by the judiciary in order to decide cases which one might normally expect to be decided on the grounds of the equality provision in Article 40.1. In *O'B v. S*[263] the Court upheld a legislative

253. [1993] 2 IR 305.
254. [1981] ILRM 324.
255. *Ibid.* 326.
256. Unreported Judgment (Supreme Court, 21 Dec. 1957).
257. *See* Casey (n. 84) 469 where he notes '[b]ut logically there would seem to be only one class – persons whose extradition is sought – and prima facie they should all receive equal treatment.'
258. *Norris* (n. 32).
259. *Ibid.*
260. *Ibid.* 59.
261. *De Búrca* (n. 236).
262. Unreported Judgment (High Court, 26 Jul. 1984).
263. [1984] IR 316.

provision which only granted rights to children of married couples in the event of intestacy. The Court pointed to the provisions of Article 41 (which identifies family rights as being especially strongly protected under the constitution) and the prevailing jurisprudence on that subject (which only recognizes and safeguards the marital family) to allow the Court to find that such distinctions were constitutionally justified. The oft-criticized Article 41.2 which recognized the role played by women within the 'home'[264] has also been used on a number of occasions to justify the preferential treatment that is afforded to married women over married men regarding gendered variations in social welfare and benefit allocations.[265]

214. Other constitutional provisions have also been used to strike down legislation to prevent sole reliance on Article 40.1. In *De Búrca*[266] perhaps the most crucial factor of the decision was not Article 40.1 but rather the right to trial by jury enshrined in Article 38.5. This right was held to mean a fully representative jury rather than a jury which had a gendered bias when it came to the pool of eligible jurors. In *Murphy v. Attorney General*[267] a taxation provision which discriminated against married couples compared to couples who were assessed separately was struck down by the Courts. This decision was not taken on the grounds of an infringement of the equality guarantee but rather on the grounds that such a tax system constituted an unjust attack on the institution of marriage and thus breached Article 41. The differences in treatment between Irish and English speakers was addressed in the case of Ó *Beolán v. Fahy*[268] by referring to Article 8 (which deals with the State's official languages) rather than by reference to the equality provision enshrined in Article 40.1.

II. The Right to Life

215. The right to life is the most sacred of natural law rights and finds expression in Article 40.3.2° of the Irish constitution, which requires the State to protect and vindicate the right to life of every citizen. Perhaps because of the fundamental nature of the right to life there is scant detail within the provision as to what exactly is to be understood by 'life' nor any explanation of when life begins or ends. The Common Law, though the creation of homicide offences, has always recognized the inherent wrong of any killing with certain exceptions such as self-defence, the death penalty and war. There is a tepid recognition of the role played by armed conflict in the establishment of the State in the Preamble text and, at various points in the Constitution, recognition of the possibility of war. The death penalty had been a feature of the Irish Constitution in Article 40.4.5°[269] prior to an amendment in 2001 which inserted Article 15.5.2°, which places a complete prohibition on the legislature from introducing a

264. *See* discussion below on the extent of this provision.
265. *See Dennehy v. Minister for Social Welfare* (High Court, unreported, 26 Jul. 1984) and *Lowth v. Minister for Social Welfare* [1998] 4 IR 321.
266. *De Búrca* (n. 236).
267. *Murphy v. Attorney General* (n. 68).
268. [2001] 2 IR 279.
269. Although the last execution in Ireland took place in 1954 it remained a theoretical possibility to have a death penalty implemented until The Criminal Justice Act, 1990.

death penalty for any offence, regardless of the circumstances. Most judicial and legislative attention has tended to focus not on the right to life itself but rather the more controversial and moral issues surrounding the right to die and what is termed by the Irish Constitution as 'the right to life of the unborn' (discussed in detail below.)

216. The case of *Re a Ward of Court (No. 2)*[270] concerned an examination of the right to life and in particular whether this encompassed a right to die. The ward in question entered hospital for a minor medical procedure but while under general anaesthetic she suffered three cardiac events which resulted in severe brain damage. According to the expert medical evidence produced, the ward was in a near persistent vegetative State with extremely limited, if any, cognitive function. Although the ward's life was sustained by medical intervention and by way of feeding tubes for twenty-two years, her family ultimately wished for the feeding tube to be withdrawn in full knowledge that death would result. Due to the fact that the woman in question had been made a ward of Court, this meant that although the Court was sympathetic to the views of the ward's family, the sole focus for the Court had to be the ward's best interests. The Court did acknowledge that the right to life of the ward was a constitutionally protected right and 'save in exceptional circumstances'[271] that right ought to trump all other considerations. The Court ultimately ruled in favour of removing the feeding tube noting that the right to life has to, by its very nature; include a right to die a natural death, seeing as death is the natural conclusion of life. The Court also noted that the ward's 'unenumerated right' to bodily integrity was also a factor in their decision. The Court was however at pains to note that the right 'does not include the right to have life terminated or death accelerated'.[272] A crucial factor here was that no positive steps were taken to end the ward's life, rather the ward died a natural death as a result of the removal of treatment which had artificially prolonged her life.

217. The importance of the distinction made by the Court in *Re a Ward of Court* was highlighted in the more recent case of *Fleming v. Ireland.*[273] Here a woman had suffered from multiple-sclerosis for a period of fourteen years and her condition had significantly worsened during that time. Although her cognitive abilities were not impaired, the Court was presented with evidence that she could not physically commit suicide without the assistance of another. Under The Criminal Law (Suicide) Act, 1993 suicide itself is no longer considered a crime but the giving of assistance in cases of suicide is an indictable offence carrying a maximum sentence of fourteen years as per section 2(2). Fleming sought to challenge the constitutionality of section 2(2) claiming that this criminal offence infringed upon her right to die via suicide. The Court held that no such right to suicide existed holding that 'in the social order contemplated by the Constitution, and the values reflected in it that would be the antithesis of the right [to life] rather than the logical consequence of it.'[274] The Court went on to affirm the distinction that was made in *Re a Ward of Court* between taking positive steps to end a life on the one hand and ceasing intervention to artificially prolong life on the other. The Court consequently held that there was no general constitutional right to die.

270. *Re a Ward of Court* (n. 206).
271. *Ibid.* 120.
272. *Ibid.* 124.
273. [2013] IESC 19.
274. *Ibid.* para. 113.

III. The Right to Life of the Unborn

218. The right to life of the unborn is without a doubt the one constitutional issue in Ireland which has caused the most controversy and debate. As originally enacted, there was no express protection for the unborn in the Irish Constitution. Abortion was offence under section 58 of the pre-independence Offences Against the Person Act, 1861 which criminalized the procurement and carrying out of unlawful miscarriages. This statute survived independence and the enactment of the 1922 and 1937 Constitutions. Although there were some judicial pronouncements on the Right to life of the unborn in the years prior to 1983 such as in *G v. An Bord Uachtála,*[275] the issue generated limited public debate due to the continued existence of the 1861 Act and the lack of any political will to repeal the relevant laws. Although the British situation changed in 1939 with the *R. v. Bourne*[276] decision which allowed abortion in certain circumstances, this had little real impact in Ireland however. It was to be a combination of the expansion of the unenumerated rights doctrine in Ireland and constitutional developments in the United States which were to have the most profound impact on Ireland and lead directly to the Eighth Amendment of the Irish Constitution, which was simply generally known at the time as the 'pro-life' amendment.

219. With the arrival of the unenumerated rights doctrine there was new scope for judicial activism in Ireland, matters which were hitherto considered to be long-settled were suddenly open to new interpretations and development. In and around the same time, the US Supreme Court passed their judgment in *Roe v. Wade*[277] which allowed an anti-abortion statute in Texas to be declared unconstitutional on the basis of the woman's right to privacy, a right which was also unenumerated. The decision in *Roe v. Wade*[278] relied strongly on the earlier decision of *Griswold v. Connecticut*[279] where the right to privacy, and in particular marital privacy, was invoked by the US Supreme Court in order to declare Connecticut's anti-contraception 'Comstock Law' unconstitutional. When the judgment in *McGee*[280] was pronounced many speculated that, given the striking similarities between *McGee*[281] and *Griswold,*[282] that there was a chance that Ireland might have its own version of *Roe v. Wade.*[283] This speculation, combined with domestic political factors, energized pro-life and Catholic groups in Ireland who argued for specific protection for the unborn in the Irish Constitution in order to avoid the possibility of an Irish version of *Roe v. Wade.*[284] Eventually after much controversy and political manoeuvring, the text of the Eighth Amendment was put before the people.[285] Two-thirds of those voting voted in favour and the Irish

275. [1980] IR 32.
276. [1939] KB 687.
277. (1973) 410 US 113.
278. *Ibid.*
279. (1965) 381 U.S. 79.
280. *McGee* (n. 32).
281. *Ibid.*
282. *Griswold* (n. 279).
283. *Roe* (n. 277).
284. *Ibid.*
285. For more background, *see generally* Tom Hesketh, *The Second Partitioning of Ireland: The Abortion Referendum of 1983* (Brandsma Books 1990).

Constitution was amended by the insertion of Article 40.3.3°, which reads: 'The State acknowledges the Right to life of the unborn and, with due regard for the equal right to life of the mother, guarantees in its laws to respect, and, as far as practicable, by its laws to defend and vindicate that right.'

220. No definition was given as to what was understood by the term 'unborn' although the Irish language text uses the slightly less ambiguous term '*an beo gan breith*' the literal translation of which would be 'the living not yet born'. Kelly points out the inherent flaw in the logic of the amendment recognizing equal rights of the unborn and the mother by noting that 'the text tried to achieve the impossible – it expressly equated two rights which, on those rare occasions when they come into conflict, cannot be reconciled.'[286] Although the initial reaction was that the abortion issue had been resolved by the passing of the amendment, the reality since then has seen abortion and the Right to life of the unborn cause reoccurring and enduring constitutional controversy.

221. The remit of the new provision was tested in a series of cases which came before the Courts in the years immediately following the amendment. The cases concerned information being provided by 'pro-choice' groups in counselling sessions and a students' union handbook about abortion services abroad. In *Attorney General (SPUC (Ireland) Ltd.) v. Open Door Counselling Ltd.*[287] the Court held that despite the absence of any enabling legislation there was none the less a duty on the Court to act to protect the Right to life of the unborn in line with the provisions of the self-executing Article 40.3.3°. In *SPUC (Ireland) Ltd. v. Grogan (No. 1)*[288] the same pro-life group successfully obtained an injunction against a student's union to prevent them publishing a handbook which detailed the existence of abortion clinics abroad. The scope of 40.3.3° was clear, where the Right to life of the unborn was under threat the Court had to act to protect it when asked to do so. However, the entire landscape was about to change drastically within a few short years.

222. In the case of *Attorney General v. X*[289] the Court was faced with the very dilemma that Kelly refers to above. X was a 14-year-old girl who had become pregnant as the result of rape. The girl, after consulting with her parents, wished to travel to the United Kingdom to procure an abortion. Prior to doing so they enquired with forensic experts if DNA and material from the aborted foetus could be used in the future criminal trial of the alleged rapist. This request made its way to the Attorney General who felt that, in line with the judgments of the *SPUC* cases (which required the active protection of the Right to life of the unborn) he had to seek an injunction to prevent X from travelling abroad to procure an abortion. The Attorney General was subsequently granted an injunction in the High Court restraining X from foreign travel for the duration of her pregnancy on the basis of the earlier decisions. The Supreme Court however, not only reversed the High Court decision but found that in certain limited circumstances an abortion could be lawfully procured in Ireland.

223. This startling development came about as a result of the precise wording of the text of Article 40.3.3° which recognizes the equal Right to life of the unborn

286. Hogan and Whyte (n. 9) 1518.
287. [1988] I.R. 593.
288. [1989] I.R. 753.
289. *Attorney General v. X* (n. 148).

and the mother. Evidence was forthcoming from a psychologist that X was suicidal and planned to take her own life if she was forced to continue with the pregnancy. The Supreme Court held by a 4 to 1 majority (with Hederman J dissenting) that the genuine threat of suicide presented a real and substantial risk to the life of the mother and in the circumstances meant that she was entitled to access an abortion in Ireland. The key element of the Supreme Court's decision was focused on the risk to the life of X – a threat to her health would not have been sufficient grounds on which to obtain an abortion. The Right to life of the unborn, the Court held, takes precedence over all rights of the mother save her right to life, as the right to life of the mother must triumph as a matter of biological pragmatism. McCarthy J summed up this line of reasoning when he noted that where 'there is a real and substantial risk attached to [maternal] survival not merely at the time of application but in contemplation at least ... throughout the pregnancy, then it may not be practicable to vindicate the Right to life of the unborn.'[290]

224. The Court also ruled in *X* that since an abortion was legally permissible in these circumstances, the Court could not subsequently prevent X from travelling to the UK for such a procedure. The Court went on to draw particular attention to the legislature's failure to pass legislation in this area since the passing of the Eighth Amendment, however it would be a further twenty-eight years before any enactment from the *Oireachtas* dealing with the substantive issue of abortion was emerge.

225. The impact of the *X* decision was profound. In the years that followed, there have been: numerous subsequent cases, challenges, campaigns to both row back and expand the remit of the decision, four further proposed referendums on related matters and European law interventions (discussed further below). The proposed Twelfth Amendment sought to reverse much of the Supreme Court's ruling in *X*[291] by excluding the threat of suicide to the life of the mother as a ground for abortion. The Thirteenth and Fourteenth Amendments specified that the general prohibition of abortion in the Article would not limit the freedom to travel within or outside of the State nor would it limit the right to distribute information about abortion services legally available abroad. The people rejected the proposed Twelfth Amendment but accepted the Thirteenth and Fourteenth amendments.[292] Legislation specifically designed to enable the regulation of the provision of information with regards to abortion services was referred to the Supreme Court by the President through use of the referral method found in Article 26[293] but was held to be constitutional in the case of *Re Article 26 and the Regulation of Information (Services outside the State for Termination of Pregnancies) Bill 1995*.[294]

290. *Ibid.* 80.
291. X (n. 148).
292. The three proposed amendments were voted on in separate referendums on the same day. It is for this reason (the rejection of the Twelfth amendment and the acceptance of the Thirteenth and Fourteenth constitutional amendments) that Ireland has no Twelfth amendment but has an Eleventh and a Thirteenth amendment.
293. *See* above paras 82–85.
294. [1995] 1 I.R. 1.

226. In the latter case of *A. and B. v. Eastern Health Board,*[295] the facts were very similar to *X*. Here however, the parents of the pregnant victim were utterly opposed to the victim procuring an abortion. The teenage mother was under the care of the State and was suicidal. The Court applied the *X* rationale and held that once there was a real and substantial risk to the life of the mother (which included a potential suicide) the right to an abortion was firmly established.

227. A fourth proposed amendment was put to the people in 2002. This proposal again looked to remove the threat of suicide as a ground for a lawful abortion and also sought to append implementing legislation to the Constitution.[296] This proposal was narrowly rejected by the people by popular vote and represented the last serious legislative engagement with the issue for a considerable period of time.

228. Two more recent events however combined to bring the issue into sharper focus and resulted in legislative action eventually being taken, a full twenty-five years after the *X* decision. In *A, B and C v. Ireland,*[297] a case was taken to the European Court of Human Rights by a non-Irish citizen concerning the difficulty she experienced in accessing and obtaining information on the circumstances in which a legal abortion was possible in Ireland. The ECtHR held that Ireland's failure to bring forward legislation clarifying the circumstances under which abortions are legally permissible violated Article 8 of the ECHR which protects private and family life. It is important to note that the judgment in *A, B and C v. Ireland*[298] did not confer a general right to abortion nor does the ECtHR have any jurisdiction to interpret the Irish Constitution. The case turned rather on the fact that there was no clear information on how the existing right, recognized in *X*, was to be accessed. The judgment, along with controversy surrounding the death of a young dentist, Savita Halappanavar in 2012,[299] led to a public outcry. The legislature reacted by enacting The Protection of Life During Pregnancy Act, 2013, which provided clarity, for the first time, as to the circumstances in which an abortion is permitted once the real and substantial risk to the life of the mother has been established and where the only course of action to eliminate that risk is the termination of a pregnancy. The three circumstances where pregnancy termination is permitted are:

(1) immediate medical emergency (which must be certified by one doctor);
(2) medical illness (which must be certified by two doctors); or
(3) risk of loss of life through suicide (which must be certified by three doctors, two of whom must be psychiatrists).

---

295. [1998] 1 I.R. 464.
296. This proposal was wholly unique in Irish Constitutional terms. The proposed legislation would have been essentially attached onto the text of the Constitution and could only have been subsequently amended or repealed by way of referendum.
297. [2010] ECHR 2032.
298. *Ibid.*
299. The case concerned a pregnant woman who was denied an abortion by doctors after she went into an early labour only 17 weeks into her pregnancy. This impasse led to a rapid deterioration in her situation and to her eventual death by sepsis – *see The Irish Times* (Dublin, 14 Nov. 2012).

229. The Right to life of the unborn is not limited merely to abortion cases however most of the attention seems to have been focused there.[300] In *Roche v. Roche*,[301] the case concerned the status of frozen embryos following a relationship breakup. The Court held that frozen embryos did not fall under the ambit of 'the unborn' as stipulated in Article 40.3.3° due to a lack of physical connection associated with implantation. In *PP v. Health Services Executive*,[302] questions arose regarding the limits of Article 40.3.3° in a case which concerned a woman who was in the early stages of her pregnancy but who had also suffered a brain death and was only being kept alive through medical intervention. The Court ruled that the life support could be removed in these circumstances, invoking the 'as far as practicable' clause of Article 40.3.3°, as expert evidence suggested there was virtually no chance of unborn surviving. However, the Court did reiterate the primacy of the Right to life of the unborn in general and went on to hint that if this pregnancy had been a bit further advanced, a much more different decision might have been reached.

230. The future development and viability of Article 40.3.3° is currently under scrutiny by the Government who have committed to examining the issue in a citizen's assembly. Considerable attention has been focused around whether abortions should be permissible in cases where there is no risk to the life of the mother but where there is no prospect of viability of the pregnancy – the so-called fatal foetal abnormality cases. Although there have been many calls and even some attempts to legislate[303] for such a factual scenario, it is difficult to see any possible viable resolution to this issue without either the repeal or the amendment of Article 40.3.3°.[304]

IV. The Right to Liberty and Due Process

231. The rights to liberty and due process are protected by the Irish Constitution in a number of ways. The right to liberty itself is expressly protected by Article 40.4.1°, which notes that: '[n]o citizen shall be deprived of his liberty save in accordance with the law'. Although the qualification would seem to suggest that the right to liberty could be easily extinguished, judicial interpretation has tended towards a strong interpretation of the right. For a variety of historic reasons and contemporary political issues at the time of the coming into force of the Irish Constitution, significant emphasis was placed upon the constitutional status of *habeas corpus* procedures. A very significant proportion of the members of the legislature in 1936 had spent considerable periods either incarcerated or interned during both the Irish revolutionary period and the subsequent Irish Civil War.

---

300. *See for example* the case of *Baby O. v. Minister for Justice* [2002] 2 I.R. 169 where the Court was very quick to dismiss the Article 40.3.3° arguments that were submitted by an embattled pregnant mother facing deportation from Ireland.
301. [2010] 2 I.R. 321.
302. [2014] IEHC 622.
303. *See for example* the unsuccessful Thirty-fifth Amendment of the Constitution (Repeal of the Eighth Amendment) Bill 2016 [Private Members Bill] (Number 56 of 2016).
304. *See* para. 329.

Persons who are arrested or otherwise deprived of their liberty have their civil rights protected by the Irish Constitution to varying degrees.

A. Rights on Arrest

232. The rights of an accused person who has been arrested are protected as a result of Article 40.4.1°. However, the rights and processes involved are strongly rooted in the Common Law tradition. Accused persons have the right upon arrest to be charged before the Courts in an expeditious manner. This charge usually takes place in the District Court which is a court of local and limited jurisdiction. The Courts have laid down a number of steps which must be taken to ensure the vindication of the rights of the accused. In *The People (DPP) v. Walsh*[305] it was held that a suspect must be informed of the offences he is being charged with when arrested. Arrests are not to be used as 'fishing expeditions' and should only be used in order to bring an accused before the Courts to face a charged offence. In *The People (DPP) v. Higgins*[306] a suspect was initially arrested for a road traffic offence but was later charged with a number of other offences as a result of statements that were made by him when he was unlawfully held in prolonged custody for the road traffic offence. The statements were deemed inadmissible by the Court due to a deliberate extension of custody beyond what was actually required to deal with the initial offence. A number of legislative exceptions do however exist which permit detentions for questioning, particularly in the area of alleged offences relating to terrorism and the illegal drugs trade.[307] The constitutionality of these kinds of legislative provisions was upheld by the Court in *The People (DPP) v. Quilligan (No. 1).*[308]

233. The questioning of a suspect must not be overly oppressive. *The People (DPP) v. Healy*[309] has stipulated that the accused possesses a right of access to counsel and to fair treatment at all times. Excessive questioning for a prolonged period without interruption can be held, as it was in *The People (DPP) v. Lynch,*[310] to invalidate a confession. Accused persons are entitled to receive any medical treatment that they require and are also entitled to be given regular food and water.

B. Right to Silence

234. The right to silence is a right which is protected under Article 38.1 of the Irish Constitution, which declares that '[n]o person shall be tried on any criminal charge save in due course of law.' This has been held to encompass the right to silence. Although there are some similarities with the United States' Fifth Amendment there are some key differences. While the Courts have accepted that a general right to silence

305. [1980] IR 294.
306. Unreported judgment of the Supreme Court, 22 Nov. 1985.
307. *See* The Offences Against the State Act, 1939 and Criminal Justice Act, 2006 for examples.
308. [1987] ILRM 606.
309. [1990] ILRM 313.
310. [1982] IR 64. *See also The People (DPP) v. Shaw [1982]* IR 1 where a confession given by an accused while intoxicated was deemed inadmissible in court.

does exist in *Heaney v. Ireland*[311], they have held that this right is not an absolute one and that circumstances do exist which can limit the qualified right to silence in Ireland. Ordinarily a person's silence cannot be used to impute their guilt; however certain legislative provisions in Irish law allow inferences to be made from a person's silence. These exceptions typically fall within the areas of alleged terrorism or illegal drug trafficking offences. Such inferences can be typically drawn from a suspect's silence when other corroborating evidence is presented. Thus in *Rock v. Ireland*[312] where a suspect was arrested and refused to speak, certain inferences could be drawn from his silence on the basis of substantiating physical evidence which linked him to the crime under investigation. The Courts have upheld these exceptions as a constitutional limitation of the right to silence on the basis that they are of benefit to the public good in the limited circumstances in which they operate. It is highly unlikely however that a broader limitation on the right to silence which covers all offences indiscriminately would be considered constitutional.

C. Bail

235. Prior to 1997, the issue of bail release presented a real issue for Irish Courts. While suspects could be detained when awaiting trial, the circumstances allowing for this were extremely limited. Only in situations where evidence could be tendered that a suspect posed a serious flight risk or where evidence indicated that the suspect was likely to intimidate key witnesses could bail be refused. The Court had even previously held in *Ryan v. DPP*[313] that bail was not to be seen as a preventative measure for stopping suspects from potentially reoffending. In *The People (DPP) v. Carmody*,[314] the Court emphasized that to do this would effectively amount to prejudging the fate of an accused that was legitimately entitled to be considered innocent until proven guilty. This problem was then remedied by the passing of the Sixteenth Amendment to the Constitution, which inserted Article 40.4.6° – a provision that allows for the denial of bail to a suspect 'where it is reasonably considered necessary to prevent the commission of a serious offence by that person.'

D. Due Process Considerations

236. Article 15.5.1° places a prohibition on passing legislation which criminalizes or prohibits any retrospective behaviour or act. Such behaviours or acts can only be classified as criminal offences after the legislation has passed into law. In *Doyle v. An Taoiseach*,[315] a taxation provision which intended to have retrospective effect was deemed to only have prospective effect by the Courts to avoid offending Article 15.5.1°.

237. Many of the long established Common Law protections for suspects find expression through Article 38.1 which requires that no person can be tried for a criminal

311. [1994] 3 IR 593.
312. [1997] 3 IR 484.
313. [1989] IR 399.
314. [1988] ILRM 370.
315. [1986] ILRM 693.

charge without '… due course of law'. In *State (Healy) v. Donoghue*,[316] the Court held that the importance of these rights protections was not in any way diminished by the fact that they are derived from the general provisions of Article 38.1 and not from an expressly provision.

238. While the presumption of innocence is a cornerstone of the Irish criminal justice system, the Courts have held, on a number of occasions that evidential burdens (but crucially not the onus of proof itself) can be shifted.[317] Innovative solutions which do shift the burden, such as the asset forfeiture provisions that were introduced by The Proceeds of Crime Act, 1996 have also been upheld as constitutional on the basis that they concern civil matters as opposed to criminal convictions.

239. Suspects should be tried in a prompt manner. The Courts have shown a real willingness to dismiss criminal cases against suspects where unreasonable delays have occurred. In *State (O'Connell) v. Fawsit*,[318] charges were dismissed after an unaccountable delay of over four years. The Court has recognized however that in certain circumstances it not always possible to bring a suspect before the Courts in a timely manner, particularly in cases of historic sexual abuse. In *PC v. DPP*,[319] the Court held that factors such as the disparity in age between the accused and the alleged victim and the perceived threats that were made to the alleged victim, (be they actual or implied) were both valid factors which would have to be taken into account when it was deciding on whether or not to excuse a lengthy case delay.

240. The accused has the right to be present at their own trial and to fully understand both the charges and trial in a language that they understand themselves. Accused persons may generally only be tried *in abstentia* in cases where they have absconded or where they do not attend the trial for reasons of their own making. In *The People (Attorney General) v. Kelly*,[320] a trial continued in the absence of an accused after he absconded from custody at the start of the trial, however in the case of *The Minister for Justice. Equality and Law Reform v. McCague*[321] the Court took the opportunity to re-emphasize that trials and sentence hearings should only be conducted *in abstentia* when extreme circumstances present.

241. Accused persons are entitled to understand court proceedings and are entitled to a translation in the event that they cannot understand the language in which the case is being conducted. The Court held this to be a function of natural justice in *The State (Buchan) v. Coyne.*[322] In *Attorney General v. Joyce and Walsh*,[323] the Court held that speakers of either one of the two official State languages (Irish or English) enjoy a 'double right' to have matters explained to them in the language of their choice, both as a function of natural justice and as a result of Article 8 which gives official status to both languages.

---

316. *State (Healy) v. Donoghue* (n. 197).
317. *See O'Leary v. Attorney General* [1993] 1 IR 102.
318. [1986] IR 362 – this case was further compromised by the unavailability of a key witness due to the passage of time.
319. [1999] 2 IR 25.
320. [2005] 1 ILRM 19.
321. [2010] IR 456.
322. (1936) 70 ILTR 185.
323. [1929] IR 526.

242. The right to jury trial in criminal matters is guaranteed under Article 38.5, albeit with a number of constitutionally mandated exceptions. Minor offences can be tried in courts of summary jurisdiction (typically the District Court) without a jury – as per Article 38.2. Special Courts, which hear cases that ordinary courts cannot deal with, are permitted by virtue of Article 38.3.1°. The Special Criminal Court has been established as a result of this provision and sits as a non-jury criminal Court in cases involving alleged terrorism and organized crime.[324] In trials where a jury is mandatory, it must be a jury of the accused's peers and should ideally be representative of society as a whole. Thus legislation which effectively served to severely limit the number of women that could serve on a jury bench was struck down in *De Búrca v. Attorney General*[325] as an unconstitutional restriction on the jury pool while *Ó Maicín v. Éire*[326] saw an accused's request for an Irish speaking jury rejected on the grounds that such a jury pool would be so restrictive as to effectively exclude the vast majority of the people living in Ireland.

E. Habeas Corpus

243. A detailed *habeas corpus* procedure is to be found from Article 40.4.2° through to Article 40.4.5°. The procedure, which has its roots in the Common Law, allows a detained person to bring an application before the Courts to inquire as to the grounds of their detention. The inquiry must take place promptly and the onus is on the person or persons responsible for the detention to prove that the detention is lawful. In *The State (Whelan) v. Governor of Mountjoy Prison,*[327] the Court placed a great deal of emphasis on the need for a prompt hearing of cases but also said that this should not be at the expense of a full, proper and detailed inquiry. If a Court is not satisfied that a person is being detained legally they have it within their power to order an immediate release. Actions can be taken against both the State and private parties.

244. The exact limits and scope of *habeas corpus* procedures in Irish law remains slightly difficult to establish, mainly due to the host of options and procedures that are open to those who wish to challenge their detention. The options include, but are in no way limited to: an action under Common Law or pre-independence legislation, an action enforcing the procedure outlined in the Constitution or a simple judicial review. Despite their differences, all these procedures share the vindication of the right to liberty at their core.

V. Freedom of Expression, Assembly and Association

245. Freedom of expression is one of the core features of a modern democracy and is given form in Article 40.6.1° (i) of the Constitution. This Article recognizes the right itself and provides a rather lengthy and detailed qualification of the right. Freedom of expression is described as a freedom for citizens to freely express their 'convictions

324. *See* para. 144.
325. *De Búrca* (n. 236).
326. [2014] IESC 12.
327. [1983] ILRM 52.

and opinions'. However, this right, like the rights of freedom of assembly and association are subject to public order and morality. The Article goes on to note that while media and press play an important role in encouraging and facilitating the freedom of expression (including criticism of the Government) such fora should not be used to undermine public order, morality or the authority of the State. Finally, there is an additional stipulation that the utterance or publication of blasphemous, seditious or indecent material is an offence, although there is no definition of this offence tendered and the regulation of this offence is left up to the legislature's discretion.

246. Although the Constitution uses the expression 'convictions and opinions' the Court in *Murphy v. Independent Radio and Television Commission*,[328] broadly interpreted this as including statements of fact and the grounds for convictions. In *The Irish Times v. Ireland*,[329] a case which concerned the reporting restrictions on certain criminal trials, the Court held that freedom of the press was guaranteed by Article 40.6.1° and that any limiting of the right of freedom of expression was an ambit which really needed to be exercised with extreme caution.

247. However, the State has limited the freedom of expression in certain circumstances, such as when the public utterance of certain views is likely to cause grave offence or result in a breach of the peace. Normally, in these circumstances legislation is enacted to regulate and occasionally criminalize such utterances, like The Prohibition on Incitement to Hatred Act, 1989 which concerns hate speech or The Criminal Justice Public Order Act, 1994 which covers 'threatening, abusive or insulting words'. In *The State (Lynch) v. Cooney*,[330] a legislative ban on the broadcasting of interviews from a political party with close ties to an illegal paramilitary grouping was upheld as a legitimate interference with the freedom.

248. The offences created by Article 40.6.1° are controversial and have been the subject of much legal analysis. In *Corway v. Independent Newspapers*,[331] a private prosecution was initiated by a citizen on foot of a cartoon published in the Respondent's newspaper which was allegedly blasphemous. The Court held that there was no workable definition available as to what exactly was to be understood by such a subjective term as blasphemy and consequently dismissed the prosecution. The legislature has since passed legislation which defines blasphemy in The Defamation Act 2009, although it should be noted that this legislative provision was drafted in such a way as to discourage its use. The Constitutional Convention has also recommended that the offence of blasphemy be removed from the text entirely.[332]

249. The freedom of association is also protected by the terms of Article 40.6.1° (iii). It protects the different forms of association, which are subject to legal regulation in the public interest. However under Article 40.6.2°, such lawfully regulated associations cannot contain discrimination on grounds of political ideology, religion or class. In *NUR v. Sullivan*,[333] the Court struck down a legislative provision which effectively granted a monopoly on union membership (in certain kinds of professions) to specific

328. [1998] 2 ILRM 360.
329. [1998] 1 IR 359.
330. *The State (Lynch) v. Cooney* (n. 237).
331. [2000] 1 ILRM 246.
332. *See* para. 325.
333. [1947] IR 77.

pre-approved trade unions on the grounds that the monopoly prohibited citizens from freely associating and forming their own unions. An equally important element of the right to associate is of course the converse right to not associate. In *Meskell v. CIÉ*,[334] the Court held that an attempt by an employer to force all of the employees under their command to join a particular trade union in order to continue on in their employment with the company was an unjust interference with the right to dis-associate.

250. The freedom of assembly is protected by Article 40.6.1° (ii) but just like the other freedoms in Article 40.6 is subject to very significant qualification and curtailment in the name of public order and morality. An emphasis is placed upon ensuring that any assembly be unarmed and regulated in accordance with law. Meetings and assemblies which are deemed to be a danger or nuisance to the public can be legally banned or curtailed. Meetings in the vicinity of *Oireachtas* buildings can also be regulated. Meetings and assemblies must be peaceful and not held to promote any unlawful act or organization. Section 27 of The Offences Against the State Act, 1939 allows for the banning of such unlawful meetings by the Gardaí, subject to review by the Courts. Picketing as part of an industrial action can raise concerns as to its legality. The Industrial Relations Act, 1990 allows for the peaceful assembly of striking workers provided that all the statutory notice periods and other technical requirements have been complied with and a nuisance or obstruction is not caused by the picket.

§3. Family Rights

I. Protection of the Family

251. Article 41 is unequivocal in its use of natural law language when it comes to the recognition of the role of the family as the 'natural and primary fundamental unit group' of Irish society and in its undertaking to protect it from 'unjust attack'. In a constitutional sense, Article 41.3 and subsequent jurisprudence makes it clear that the family referred to in Article 41 is the marital family. This was touched upon in *The State (Nicolaou) v. An Bord Uchtála*[335] which discussed the legal nature of families. The Court made it clear that an unmarried father of a child would not be considered part of a family in the constitutional sense of the term and any rights they possess were rooted in legislation. While unmarried mothers are not able to avail of family rights either, they do enjoy 'unenumerated rights' (vis-à-vis their child) which are essentially akin to family rights under Article 41. It is worth noting in the case of unmarried mothers however that the rights recognized under Article 40.3 are not couched in the same kind of natural law language that is clearly evidenced in the Article 41 provision. This effectively means that the State is only obliged to vindicate these surrogate rights 'as far as [is reasonably] practicable'. There is however no requirement that the married couple must have children to be able to avail of their right to a family life as per *Murray v. Ireland.*[336]

334. [1973] IR 121.
335. [1966] IR 567.
336. *Murray* (n. 54).

252. The ambit of the protection offered to a family was demonstrated in the case of *Murphy v. Attorney General*,[337] where a taxation provision in The Finance Act, 1978 was struck down as unconstitutional. The Act prescribed a new taxation system which had the effect of giving an unmarried couple who were assessed separately a more advantageous position than that of a married couple who were jointly assessed. The Court struck down the new arrangement as an unjust attack on the family and the institution of marriage. A similar case which followed this reasoning was *Hyland v. Minister for Social Welfare*,[338] where a social welfare provision which treated unmarried cohabiting couples more favourably than married couples was struck down on roughly the same grounds. The important element in both of these cases was the fact that the couples in the non-marital unions were being treated more favourably than their married counterparts. There is however no impediment to the equal treatment of marital and non-marital unions within the actual text of the Constitution.

II. Marriage

253. Traditionally, the Irish understanding of marriage was that of a heterosexual union between a man and a woman for life. However, a number of constitutional amendments have since changed this position. Prior to 1996, the Constitution expressly forbade any legislation which would provide for divorce, however the Fifteenth Amendment allowed for the dissolution of marriages in certain prescribed circumstances as per the amended Article 41.3.2°. The situation with respect to same sex marriage was somewhat different as an outright prohibition on same-sex marriage did not exist in the constitutional text itself but was an ingrained part of the Common Law and judicial interpretation. In *Zappone v. Revenue Commissioners*[339] the traditional heterosexual definition of marriage was upheld by the Court, which pointed to recent legislative enactments which confirmed that the traditional understanding of marriage was still a correct reading of the Constitution. This situation was changed by the Thirty-Fourth Amendment which inserted a new provision, Article 41.4 which now allows for marriage 'contracted in accordance with law by two persons without distinction as to [their] sex.'

III. The Role of Women

254. Article 41.2, which speaks of the role of women within the home is one of the more controversial provisions of the Constitution and is widely criticized as being out of date and in need of reform. This Article reads as follows:

> 1° In particular, the State recognises that by her life within the home, woman gives to the State a support without which the common good cannot be achieved.

337. *Murphy v. Attorney General* (n. 68).
338. [1989] IR 624.
339. [2008] 2 IR 417.

2° The State shall, therefore, endeavour to ensure that mothers shall not be obliged by economic necessity to engage in labour to the neglect of their duties in the home.

Kelly describes the provision as perhaps 'the single most dated provision of the Constitution.'[340] If the motivation behind the inclusion of this provision was to give economic protection to women or to prevent them having to work against their wishes, then the provision has failed miserably. As the Constitutional Review group notes that the provision has failed to have any significant impact towards achieving this aim.[341] The provision is often cited as being both insulting and denigrating to women.

255. However, Denham J. has offered a different view. She has suggested that the provision has to be read in light of the changing role of women in society. She stated in *Sinnott v. Minister for Education* that, 'this recognition and acknowledgement does not exclude women and mothers from other roles and activities. It is a recognition of the work performed by women in the home. The work is recognised because it has immense benefit for society.'[342] The Irish language text of the Constitution does in fact offer some justification for this position, as the Irish expression '*teaghlach*', which literally translates into English as household, is used in place of home and could perhaps be said to encompass a much broader understanding of the positive role that is played by women in society.

256. The citizen-led Constitutional Convention recommended in 2013 that Article 41.2 be replaced with a more gender-neutral provision that recognizes the contribution of all carers in the home but no further progress has been made on this issue since the recommendation was made.

IV. The Rights of the Child

257. The rights of the child were traditionally seen as being best protected within the ambit of family rights as per the decision in *Re JH (An Infant).*[343] Here, Finlay CJ said that there is 'a constitutional presumption that the welfare of the child … is to be found within the family, unless the Court is satisfied on the evidence that there are compelling reasons why this cannot be achieved, or unless the Court is satisfied that the evidence establishes an exceptional case where the parents have failed to provide education for the child and continue to fail to provide education for the child for moral or physical reasons.'[344] Thus, the rights of the child were essentially bound up with the rights of the marital family. While there was some limited reference to the rights of the child in the former Article 42.5 there was no explicit definition as to the nature of these rights. In *G v. An Bord Uchtála*[345] the Court gave a non-exhaustive list of rights that children have, including but not limited to: the right to be fed, the right to

340. Hogan and Whyte (n. 9).
341. The Constitutional Review Group (n. 233) 311.
342. *Sinnot v. Minister for Education* (n. 73) 665.
343. [1985] IR 375.
344. *Ibid.* 395.
345. *G v. An Bord Uchtála* (n. 55).

live, the right to be reared, the right to be educated and the right to realize their full potential. All these rights were presumed to be best protected within the family unit. This meant that judges felt constrained by the Constitution in their decisions. For example, in the case of *N v. Health Service Executive*[346] (better known as the 'Baby Ann case') an unmarried couple had given their baby up for adoption only to subsequently change their minds and get married. The Supreme Court felt that because the Constitution gives such priority to the marital family it had to decide the case in favour of the marital parents because there had been no serious failures on their part., This was despite the fact that the baby had been with its prospective adoptive parents for a period of twenty-four months at the time of the hearing. The case indicates of the lack of consideration shown for the welfare concerns of children when their rights are subsumed within the marital family unit.

258. In *North Western Health Board v. HW*,[347] the parents of a child refused permission for a heel prick test to be carried out on their child shortly after its birth due to their belief that no pain should ever be inflicted on a child. The test is a standard medical procedure used to screen for a number of genetic and developmental conditions. The State sought permission to carry out the test without parental consent. The Court held that the parents' refusal of consent was permitted and that the State could only intervene in cases where there was a grave and immediate threat to the welfare of a child. However, in *Re Baby AB*[348] the Court authorized an intervention by the State in a case where a lifesaving blood transfusion was required by a child in spite of their parents' objections on religious grounds.

259. The Thirty-First Amendment of the Constitution was approved by the people in a referendum in November 2012 but only became law in 2015 after a number of unsuccessful challenges were taken to the result on foot of an illegal interference in the referendum process by the Government.[349]

260. The previous provision, Article 42.5, fell under the ambit of Article 42 and was entitled 'Education'. It concerned not only the rights of the child but parental failure and was not merely confined to the educational sphere. This Article was removed and the new, more detailed Article 42A replaced it. The new Article expressly references the 'natural and imprescriptible' rights of the child. The Article also enshrined the welfare principle (which only had legislative recognition up until that point) on a constitutional basis and allowed for State intervention in exceptional cases of parental failure. Article 42A allows for the voluntary adoption of children that are born to married parents (something which was previously not permitted) and finally, the new Article makes provision for the views of children to be heard in court cases that concerned their safety and welfare, with due weight being given to the relative age and maturity of the respective child.

346. [2006] IESC 60.
347. [2001] 3 IR 622.
348. [2011] 1 IR 665.
349. *See* para. 34.

§4. Education Rights

I. Family Rights and Education

261. Article 42 deals with education and is a provision that is very much intertwined with the preceding Article on the family, evidencing similar natural law language. The Family is described as the 'natural and primary' educator in Article 42.1 and as such has certain rights and duties imposed upon it with regards the provision of education. Article 42.1 refers to education in the broadest sense of the term, encompassing religious, moral, physical and social education.

262. The only part of Article 42 where a particular level of education is expressly specified is Article 42.4. It refers to a right to free primary education. As a consequence the existing constitutional jurisprudence on education focuses almost exclusively on primary education and does not include secondary or tertiary education, which is instead regulated by legislation.

263. Article 42.2 allows parents to home-school their children or to send their children to schools run either privately or by the State. While this would appear to give parents a great degree of choice in where to send their children to school, in practice the choices are somewhat limited due to the scarce number of non-denominational and multidenominational faith schools in Ireland. Furthermore, Article 42.3.1° makes it clear that no parent shall be forced to send their children to schools that are either 'established or designated by the State'. In practice however, over 90% of the primary schools in Ireland are private schools run by religious organizations, therefore this choice can be greatly limited. These schools, although in the ownership of and run under the patronage of religious organizations, tend to be funded by the State. Article 44 (although primarily concerned with religion) specifies in paragraph 4 that children attending schools which are under religious patronage but State funded can be excused from religious instruction if their parents so wish. However, in *Campaign to Separate Church and State Ltd. v. Minister for Education*[350] the Court recognized that children cannot be entirely excluded from the religious ethos of their particular school.[351]

264. Private education bodies have a great deal of autonomy in how they choose to run their schools, however the State is obliged by Article 42.3.2° to ensure that a 'certain minimum education' is provided. This provision has led to some significant case law in the area which explores what academic standard a 'certain minimum education' imposes. In the case of *O'Shiel v. Minister for Education*,[352] parents had established a private school which the State had refused to fund. This decision was based on that fact that the school's teachers lacked the relevant qualifications usually needed to educate children and the level of Irish language education that was provided by the school was severely deficient. The Court recognized that the State was in fact entitled to link the provision of its funding to the attainment of a basic level of 'certain

350. [1998] 3 IR 321.

351. *See* further Conor O'Mahony, 'Religious Liberty in the Irish Education System' in Derek Davies & Elena Miroshnikova (eds), *The Routledge International Handbook of Religious Education* (Routledge 2012).

352. [1999] 2 ILRM 241.

minimum education'. In the case of *DPP v. Best*,[353] the Court held that although a failure to teach the full curriculum was not, by itself, a failure to attain the 'certain minimum education' standard, it was usually indicative of a failure to reach it .

II. Free Primary Education

265. Article 42.4 is one of the only unfettered rights within the Irish Constitution and confers a right to free primary education, which the State must provide for. The expression 'provide *for*' is crucial here – the State can, and in over 90% of cases it does, in effect franchise out the provision of free primary education to private organizations, most of which are religious. The Court acknowledged in *Crowley v. Ireland*[354] that while the State cannot wash their hands of the obligation to provide free primary education once such education is being provided by a private organization, the State cannot be said to be failing in its constitutional duty towards children once adequate steps to provide for free primary education are taken. Casey criticizes this decision as a validation of '[m]inisterial inactivity'.[355] In the subsequent case of *Sinnott v. Minister for Education*[356] however, the Court appeared to shift their emphasis, by suggesting that the State needs to take a 'hands-on approach' in order to ensure that their obligations under Article 42.4 were fully complied with.

266. Although Article 42.4 fails to define what 'free primary education' actually means, the area of special education needs has led to some much more detailed examination of the issue.[357] In *O'Donoghue v. Minister for Health*,[358] the Court held that the duty to provide for free primary education was not a 'one size fits all' approach and that the State was under an obligation to take account of the differences in capacity that children with special needs have. The Court expanded on this in *Comerford v. Minister for Education*,[359] where it held that a child with attention deficit disorder was not having his constitutional right to primary education vindicated by the State. The key element here was the Court's view that there was a duty upon the State to vary the education provided in conjunction with the needs and abilities of the child.

267. In *Sinnott v. Minister for Education*,[360] a question arose as to the nature and extent of free primary education. The Plaintiff suffered from a severe disability which greatly impacted upon his ability to avail of primary education. Special needs education was provided and the Plaintiff benefitted from the education and, as a result, his quality of life improved. A question did arise however, as to what the upper age limit was and at what stage the State no longer had a duty to provide for a citizen's free primary education.

353. [2000] 2 IR 17.
354. [1980] IR 102.
355. Casey (n. 84) 658.
356. *Sinnot v. Minister for Education* (n. 73).
357. *See generally* Conor O'Mahony, *Educational Rights in Irish Law* (Thomson Round Hall 2006).
358. [1996] 2 IR 20.
359. [1997] 2 ILRM 134.
360. *Sinnot v. Minister for Education* (n. 73).

268. The State argued that once the Plaintiff had progressed into adulthood they were no longer entitled to receive free primary education from the State. Although the Plaintiff was successful in the High Court, which held that free primary education should continue as long as there is a need for it, this decision was subsequently overturned by the Supreme Court on appeal. The Supreme Court instead held that primary education ceased once a citizen entered adulthood (and possibly before – the Court was not unanimous in its agreement as to the exact cut-off point). It also stated that the Plaintiff could not be considered a child for the purposes of Article 42 by virtue of his disability. The Court relied on a harmonious interpretation of Article 42 to reach its decision in this case since the term child was not actually mentioned in Article 42.4 itself but was expressly alluded to under Article 42.

269. The quality of the special needs education that the State is obliged to provide was examined in *O'Carolan v. Minister for Education.*[361] The Plaintiff's parents wished for the State to pay for special needs education abroad which was of a perceived higher quality than the domestic education the Plaintiff was receiving in Ireland. The Court was satisfied however that the special needs education provided in Ireland was of a sufficient standard as to discharge the State's obligations and that there was no obligation upon the State to provide for a standard of education that went both above and beyond this most basic requirement.

§5. Property Rights

270. Property Rights occupy a particularly important place in Irish law and, perhaps more significantly, in the Irish psyche. Property and landownership movements were traditionally tied to the question of Irish independence.[362] As a result, the historical context in which the Constitution was introduced is important to note. The British conquest of Ireland inevitably led to land confiscation and the payment of rents by those who lived and worked land to absentee landlords. Unusually, the 1922 Irish Free State Constitution did not enshrine a right to private property – instead Article 11 contains references to the public ownership of land and the 'natural resources' of the State. It is thought that the principle reason behind these anomalies is to be found in the influential ideas of public ownership of land and property that were predominant within f the Ancient Gaelic State, which was a strong source of inspiration for the 1922 Constitution.[363]When drafting the 1937 Constitution, the Bill of Rights was considerably expanded and property rights became a significant new addition.

271. Property rights are first mentioned in a limited sense in Article 40.3.2 where they are enshrined as personal rights which the State is obliged to protect from unjust attack. Article 43 is given the title '[p]rivate [p]roperty' and has significantly more detail. The right to privately own property is explicitly affirmed as a natural right by Article 43.1.1°. Article 43.1.2° guarantees that laws shall not be passed which abolish

361. [2005] IEHC 296.

362. *See for example*, Philip Bull, *Land, politics and nationalism: a study of the Irish land question* (Gill and MacMillan 1996) and Donald E. Jordan. *Land and popular politics in Ireland: County Mayo from the Plantation to the Land War* (Cambridge University Press 1994).

363. *See* Cahillane, *Drafting the Irish Free State Constitution* (n. 5).

the right of private ownership or the right to transfer, bequeath or inherit private property. Article 43.2.1° and 43.2.2° do however recognize that the common good can sometimes require the regulation and limitation of these rights by law. The Court has confirmed in *Dreher v. Irish Land Commission*[364] that Articles 40.3.2 and 43 are to be read in conjunction with each other and that while there is an obligation to protect property rights from unjust attack, legitimate interference with such rights is also permitted. In *Buckley v. Attorney General*[365] (better known as the *Sinn Féin* Funds case), the validity of legislation which attempted to control a fund held by a private organization was examined.

272. The Court held that Article 43.1.2° applied not merely as a general rule but also as a constitutional protection against the interference with the property rights of individual citizens and legal entities. This put them at odds with the State which had argued that the true meaning of Article 43.1.2° was the prohibition of laws which violated property rights in general rather than a ban on the violation of specific property rights themselves. In *Madigan v. Attorney General*[366] the Court confirmed that the levying of taxation was, without doubt, an interference with the property rights of all citizens but also held that it is an absolutely justifiable one which befits the common good. Likewise, in *O'Callaghan v. Commissioners of Public Works*,[367] the Court held that the preservation of a national monument was a legitimate interference with the property rights of a citizen for the common good.

273. The compulsory purchase of land for public works and the common good (provided compensation is paid), was found to be lawful in *Fisher v. Irish Land Commission.*[368] However, in *ESB v. Gormley*,[369] the absence of an independent compensation scheme was held to be an infringement of a citizen's property rights. In *Daly v. Revenue Commissioners*,[370] certain provisions within a tax statute which allowed the State to withhold additional taxes from citizens were held to be unfair, unjust and a disproportionate interference with their property rights. However, the case also held that when these property rights are infringed in this way compensation is not always required to be paid by the State. In *Gilligan v. Criminal Assets Bureau*,[371] asset forfeiture legislation which enabled the State (subject to a judicial review process) to take control of assets which it believed to be the proceeds of crime was upheld as constitutional. The case of *Clinton v. An Bord Pleanála*[372] has established however that the State has a higher evidential burden of proof to surmount than is normally the case in most civil actions when seeking to justify its interferences with the property rights of its citizens.

274. The types and classes of property protected by the Constitution are not all expressly detailed in Article 43. In addition to land, dwellings, and monies, the rights arising out of them are also understood to be afforded constitutional protection. The

364. [1984] ILRM 94.
365. [1950] IR 67.
366. [1986] ILRM 136.
367. [1985] ILRM 364.
368. [1948] IR 3.
369. [1985] IR 129.
370. [1995] 3 IR 1.
371. [1998] 3 IR 185.
372. [2007] IESC 19.

Court has further held that rights arising from pensions,[373] contractual relationships,[374] licences[375] and franchises[376] are all considered to be constitutionally protected property rights. Rent control legislation was struck down in *Blake v. Attorney General*[377] and *In Re Housing (Private Rented Dwellings) Bill 1981*[378] as an unjust restriction on the constitutional property rights of landlords due to the highly restrictive nature of the scheme. A more recent and limited attempt at rent control legislation was passed by the legislature in 2015 in the form of The Residential Tenancies (Amendment) Act, 2015 although this new scheme has yet to be challenged before the Courts.

§6. Religion

275. References to religion are found throughout the text of the Constitution. The preamble has a strong Christian focus, with references to the 'Most Holy Trinity' and 'our Devine Lord, Jesus Christ'. Article 6 notes that all powers of Government 'derive, under God, from the People' while each oath of office which is prescribed in the Constitution has a reference to God in it. Article 44 however is directly concerned with religion. The Article evidences a strongly religious tone, noting that worship is 'due to Almighty God' and that religion should be respected and honoured. These references to religion and God are perhaps best seen as a reflection of pre-war Irish society at a time when the population of the State was overwhelmingly Catholic, with the Anglican faith making up most of the remaining minority.[379] This status was officially acknowledged in Articles 44.1.2° and 44.1.3° which were both repealed in 1972. Article 44.1.2° noted the 'special position' of the Catholic Church in Ireland while Article 44.1.3° expressly acknowledged other minority Christian faiths and the Jewish community in Ireland. Precisely what impact the 'special position' and the recognition of other faiths had in a legal sense was never fully explored by the Courts. Geoghegan J argued in *Ó Beoláin v. Fahy*[380] that the provision was never intended to have any legal meaning and was instead an example of the Constitution embodying the aspirations and emotional feelings of the people who have enacted it. It has been argued however that Article 44.1 (through its acceptance of a deity) effectively amounts to the Constitution awarding a privileged status to people who profess religion as opposed to those who do not[381] although the Court has held in *Mulloy v. Minister for*

373. *Lovett v. Minister for Education* [1997] 1 ILRM 89.
374. *Hamilton v. Hamilton* [1982] IR 466.
375. *Hempenstall v. Minister for the Environment* [1994] 2 IR 20 – it should be noted that licenses in particular are often the subject of significant legitimate legislative regulation.
376. *DPP (Long) v. McDonald* [1983] ILRM 223.
377. [1982] IR 117.
378. [1983] IR 181.
379. According to the 1936 Census Catholics made up 93.44% of the population of Ireland with the Anglican Church of Ireland accounting for 4.9% of the total population.
380. *Ó Beoláin* (n. 197) 356.
381. Oran Doyle, 'Article 44: Privileging the Rights of the Religious' in Carolan and Doyle (eds), *The Irish Constitution: Governance and Values* (Thomson Round Hall 2008) 476.

Education[382] that the freedoms of the Article apply to non-believers in the same way they apply to those who follow particular faiths.

276. The Court stated in the case of *Quinn's Supermarket Ltd. v. Attorney General*[383] (a case which concerned whether more flexible opening hours were allowed for Kosher butchers to account for the Sabbath) that the main purpose of Article 44 is to guarantee the free practice of religion. Where legislative interventions are required to give effect to such free practice, those legislative provisions would be constitutional, provided that they only goes so far as is necessary to facilitate the free practice of religion. The Court also held that Article 44 was not to be read in such a way as to prevent the State from passing laws which allow for the free practice of religion.

277. In *M. v. An Bord Uchtála,*[384] legislation which required prospective adoptive parents to be the same religion as the child they wished to adopt was held to be unconstitutional discrimination. However, in *Murphy v. Independent Radio and Television Commission,*[385] legislation which effectively banned advertising of a religious nature in the broadcast media was held to be constitutional, as no one religion was discriminated against and all religions were included in the prohibition. It should be noted however that the most recent broadcasting legislation would also seem to effectively prohibit advertising which would either promote or discourage the respective merits and demerits of religious non-belief.[386]

278. Article 44 had been held as forbidding the establishment or recognition of an official State religion, as well as prohibiting the monetary support of any particular religion. However, in *Campaign to Separate Church and State v. Minister for Education,*[387] the Court held that payments by the State to teachers and chaplains in private schools did not amount to monetary support of a particular faith as the State was justified in doing so in order to provide education.

279. In recent times, questions of education and religion have garnered significant attention and focus in legislation and policy, resulting in some significant changes. For example, in the years prior to 2015, private schools run by religious organizations were given certain exemptions from equality legislation,[388] which allowed them to discriminate against prospective students in order to protect their religious ethos.[389] However this exemption was abolished by The Equality (Miscellaneous Provisions) Act, 2015. In January 2016, the controversial Rule 68 of the Rules for Primary Schools in Ireland, which prioritized religion over all other education, was abolished due to what was considered its anarchic focus and language of the provision. Issues remain however with regards to the access of education in privately run religious schools which receive State funding. Section 7 of The Equal Status Act 2000 gives these

382. [1975] IR 88.
383. *Quinn's Supermarket Ltd. v. Attorney General* (n. 76).
384. [1975] IR 81.
385. *Murphy v. Independent Radio and Television Commission* (n. 328).
386. *See* s. 41(4) of The Broadcasting Act 2009.
387. [1998] 2 ILRM 81.
388. *See* s. 37 of The Employment (Equality) Act 1998.
389. The exemption would have effectively permitted a religious school to decide not to hire a particular teacher who was openly gay on the basis that their sexuality was contrary to the ethos of the patron organization of the school.

schools the permission to discriminate in school enrolment in order to protect the religious ethos of the school. Such discrimination can result in children of a different religion to that of the school (or children of no religion) being denied places in favour of children belonging to the religious group to which the school is affiliated. There is now some discussion as to whether this too should be abolished.

Chapter 3. Constitutional Problems of Minorities

280. Ireland has, in recent years, become an increasingly multicultural and multi-ethnic society, with a 143% increase having been recorded in the number of people not born in Ireland now living in the State, according to the most recent census data.[390] Significant minorities now exist in Ireland from a number of different communities and groups; however these minorities lack any significant legal recognition as minorities *per se*. While religious minorities have long existed in Ireland, aside from a now repealed provision, there has been little recognition on this fact within the Irish legal system. The Irish language community in Ireland is a de facto minority group; however the Constitution does not recognize them as such. Indeed by nominating the Irish language as being the first official language of the State under Article 8, the Irish Constitution actually puts the Irish language and its speakers in something of an artificial position.

281. In terms of indigenous minorities present in Ireland, the only group who can claim such recognition would be the 'members of the Travelling Community', who have limited recognition as a minority group in legislation (at a sub-constitutional level see below). 'Travelling Community' interest groups have long sought for 'members of the Travelling community' to be given State recognition as an ethnic or minority group on an official governmental basis; however these efforts tend to focus their energies at the sub-constitutional level, as there are currently no constitutionally recognized minority groups in Ireland today.

282. The most significant legal instruments for protecting and naming (but not officially recognizing) minorities at a legislative level has proven to be The Prohibition on Incitement to Hatred Act 1989, The Employment Equality Act 1998 and The Equal Status Act 2000 which all prohibit discrimination and hatred on a number of grounds which include membership of minority communities (such as membership of the travelling community) and religious groups.

283. In the past, a convention[391] was observed whereby at least one member of the High or Supreme Court would come from the Protestant faith.[392] This convention arose out of a willingness to demonstrate to the Protestant minority that a place in public life was always open for that community despite the fact that independent Ireland has always been predominantly Catholic. This convention was largely observed right through, from independence through to the present day, with members of the High and Supreme Courts coming from the Catholic and Protestant faiths (and indeed even those of no faith). Due to the nature of constitutional conventions, it still remains unclear if this convention continues in existence in modern multi-cultural Ireland or whether the current make-up of the superior Courts is merely happenstance.

390. Census data 2011.

391. *See* para. 47.

392. *See* Morgan, *Constitutional Law of Ireland* (n. 15) 14.

Chapter 4. Legal Position of Foreign Nationals

284. Foreign nationals, as a group, are not expressly mentioned in the Irish Constitution. Although the Constitution repeatedly uses the expression 'citizen' when referring to fundamental rights, the Courts have held that such rights should apply to all persons by nature of their inherent humanity. However, in Article 16.1.2° (i), the right to vote in *Dáil* and related elections is restricted to citizens of Ireland. Yet Article 16.1.2° (ii) does allow for provision to be made for non-Irish citizens to vote in *Dáil* elections. Article 2 recognizes the affinity of the Nation with people of Irish ancestry living abroad but does not confer any special rights or status onto this group.

285. British nationals enjoy a number of special concessions within the Irish Constitution. This is essentially a result of the close historic and political ties between Ireland and Britain, with Northern Ireland in particular being seen as worthy of special interest. As a result of legislative provisions passed under Article 16.1.2° (ii), British nationals who are resident in Ireland can register to vote in *Dáil* elections. All persons born on the island of Ireland (including the parts of Northern Ireland that are still currently subject to British rule) are entitled, subject to certain conditions,[393] to Irish citizenship by virtue of the legislation which was passed following the signing of the 'Good Friday Agreement'. Many reciprocal agreements exist between the United Kingdom and Ireland on areas including: security, data exchange free movement and social welfare. Although a number of these agreements have been superseded by EU membership. The proposed renouncing of EU membership by the United Kingdom in the wake of the referendum that was held on 23 June 2016 could ultimately lead to further multilateral co-operation between Britain and Ireland.

286. EU citizens in Ireland enjoy all the rights normally associated with EU membership, by virtue of Ireland's membership of the EU, however these rights are limited to what is required by membership of the EU and do not extend beyond the freedoms that are afforded to all EU citizens. This status does however have a limited constitutional scope by virtue of the operation of Article 29.4.6°, which gives EU law supremacy over all Irish law, including all Irish constitutional provisions. In the event that a provision of Irish law and an EU citizen's freedom were found to be in conflict with each other, the EU citizen's freedom would have to be recognized as superior and would triumph.[394]

287. The legal status of non-Irish citizens from outside the EU and United Kingdom varies based on the treaties between Ireland and the various States in question; however such agreements all exist at a sub-constitutional level. Ireland has still nevertheless accepted the jurisdiction of a number of international courts and tribunals on a constitutional level, such as the International Criminal Court. Acceptance of the jurisdiction of the International Criminal Court (ICC) places certain obligations on Ireland vis-à-vis extradition under the Rome Statue which could potentially have a major impact on the rights of citizens of other jurisdictions in Ireland.

---

393. *See* para. 192.
394. *See* para. 188.

Chapter 5. The ECHR and Rights in Ireland

288. Ireland is a signatory of the ECHR. It is important to note however, when assessing constitutional rights, that the ECHR has never been incorporated at a constitutional level in Ireland. Although Ireland was a signatory and early adopter of the ECHR, prior to 2003 the ECHR initially had no firm statutory footing in Irish law as per the decision in *In re Ó Láighleis*.[395] When relevant cases arose during this period they were treated according to Ireland's Convention obligations. Plaintiffs who had exhausted their domestic options would be permitted to take their case to the European Court of Human Rights (ECtHR) with a view to having their Convention rights properly vindicated at an international law level. Even if a Plaintiff was eventually successful under this system, there was no domestic legal compulsion on the State that bound it to either accept the ECtHR decision or to implement its findings, but in view of its treaty obligations, the State would usually try to amend its law whenever possible.

289. The *Norris*[396] case is perhaps the best illustration of the impact of the ECHR on Ireland prior to 2003.[397] The Plaintiff was a gay man who, having failed in his attempts in the Irish Courts to have a statute which effectively criminalized homosexual activity between males declared unconstitutional, took his case to the ECtHR. His action was ultimately successful, with the ECtHR holding that the Irish statute which criminalized homosexuality was incompatible with the ECHR. However, such a declaration had no direct effect on Irish domestic law. The ECtHR did have the power to award damages against the State for the violation, but the ECtHR lacked, and still lacks, any power to expressly compel Ireland to domestically enforce its judgments. Ireland has, however, adopted a practice of compliance with the judgments of the ECtHR, deciding to amend offending legislation and practices which are found to be in breach of the State's obligations under the ECHR. As a result of the *Norris*[398] decision in the ECtHR, the *Oireachtas* decided to amend the offending legislative provision and ended the effective criminalization of homosexual acts between males in Ireland by passing The Criminal Law (Sexual Offences) Act 1993.

290. Although Ireland was one of the original countries to sign up to the ECHR in 1950, the Convention was not transposed directly into Irish law until the passing of The European Convention on Human Rights Act 2003. The signing of the Belfast Agreement[399] in 1998 included a commitment by the State to ground the ECHR into the domestic legal system in Ireland, which the State accomplished with the passing of the European Convention on Human Rights Act 2003. It should be noted however that the ECHR Act, which is an act that was passed by the legislature and thus legally incorporated at a sub-constitutional level, is still subject to all the same constitutional implications as any other piece of domestic legislation. The ECHR Act must be compatible with all aspects of the Irish Constitution; it cannot look to override any provision of the Irish Constitution and can only have effect in as much as the Irish

395. [1960] IR 93.
396. Norris (n. 168).
397. *Ibid.*
398. *Ibid.*
399. Better known as the 'Good Friday Agreement' – *see* para. 25 n 31.

Constitution allows it to. Whenever a legal conflict arises between the provisions of the ECHR Act and the Irish Constitution, it is always the Irish Constitution which must be allowed to prevail under Irish law.

291. The ECHR Act does however give domestic effect in Ireland to the provisions of the European Convention on Human Rights, allowing parties to raise ECHR considerations directly in domestic Irish courts without the need to petition the ECtHR directly or exhaust all domestic remedies first.

292. Sections 2–5 of the ECHR Act set out the manner in which the ECHR Act gives the ECHR a footing in Irish Law. Section 2 imposes an obligation on all Courts to interpret Irish law in a manner that is compatible with the ECHR and stipulates that this obligation is retrospective in effect, encompassing legislation which was already in force prior to the enactment of the ECHR Act. Section 3 creates a statutory obligation on every 'organ of the State' to act in compliance with the ECHR provisions and allows for the recovery of damages when breaches of the ECHR are found by the Courts. Section 4 provides that the Irish Courts will take 'judicial notice' of ECtHR case law when deciding cases within the domestic legal system. While section 5 sets out the mechanism for declarations of incompatibility, this is a situation which occurs when an Irish Court finds a legislative provision or legal rule to be fundamentally incompatible with the obligations of the State under the ECHR. Such a declaration of incompatibility does not render the offending provision or law void but does serve to put the State on notice that such a fundamental incompatibility exists. A declaration of incompatibility does not impact on a Plaintiff's ability to present their case to the ECtHR and avail of the appropriate remedies there.

293. The first example of a declaration of incompatibility under the ECHR Act was seen in the case of *Foy v. An t-Ard Chláraitheoir & Others.*[400] The Plaintiff was a transgender woman who had been refused a birth certificate with her new name and gender. She appealed the refusal by invoking the ECHR Act. The Irish High Court, taking notice of two similar cases in the ECtHR, (where the United Kingdom was found to be in breach of the ECHR for its failure to recognize transgender persons) held that the existing Irish citizen registration system was fundamentally incompatible with Irish obligations under the ECHR. After a significant delay the legislature eventually remedied this incompatibility by passing The Gender Recognition Act 2015 which finally remedied the failings of the previous system.

294. When it comes to the interaction between the Irish Constitution and the ECHR, the Irish Courts have emphasized that while international law obligations are to be taken seriously, such obligations can only be effected to the extent to which domestic law (rather than international law) allows.[401] Therefore, although inherent tensions are bound to arise occasionally in circumstances where both domestic and international rights obligations conflict, in the Constitutional sense there can be only one victor in such an instance – the Irish Constitution.

400. [2007] IEHC 470; [2012] 2 IR 1.

401. *See generally McD v. L* [2010] 2 IR 199.

Part V. Specific Problems

Chapter 1. War and Foreign Affairs Powers

295. According to Article 28.3, the consent of the *Dáil* is required before participation in any war. Article 15.6 also specifies that only the *Oireachtas* can 'raise and maintain military or armed forces' and any form of private army within the State is prohibited. The Defence Acts from 1954 to 2011 provide for the functioning of the defence forces in Ireland.

296. Ireland has not participated in any wars during the history of the State. Ireland is not a member of North Atlantic Treaty Organization (NATO) or any other military alliance, although the Irish Army has served under the auspices of the United Nations in peacekeeping roles. In relation to the common security and defence policy of the European Union, Article 29.4.9° provides that: 'The State shall not adopt a decision taken by the European Council to establish a common defence pursuant to Article 42 of the Treaty on European Union where that common defence would include the State.'

297. The powers of the executive in relation to foreign affairs have been discussed above.[402]

402. *See* para. 124.

Chapter 2. Public Finance / Taxation

298. The Irish Constitution sets no express fiscal targets, taxation requirements or budgetary rules. Article 11 established that a singular public fund shall exist into which the State's income (principally via taxation) and out of which the State's expenditure shall be paid. Fiscal policy however is seen as a matter in the sole domain of the Executive, with enabling legislation passed through the normal legislative process in the *Oireachtas*. As fiscal policy is considered to be a matter for the Executive, it is thus beyond the remit of the Courts to examine save for questions of procedure or implantation.

299. Articles 21 and 22 prescribe that certain bills which have financial or tax related aims shall be known as 'Money Bills'. Such bills must commence in the *Dáil* and enjoy protection from amendment, delay and rejection in the *Seanad* which is a privilege not normally afforded to other bills. In a similar vein, according to Article 28.7.1°, the Minister for Finance must be a member of the *Dáil* and cannot be a member of the *Seanad* (unlike most other ministerial offices). Article 28.4.3° requires that a budget be prepared each year and placed before the *Dáil* for consideration but again no mention is made of the *Seanad.* The special procedures extended to money bills and financial matters in the *Dáil* hint at a connection between the directly elected (and consequently more democratic) *Dáil* and control of public finance with Casey noting that the exclusion of the non-directly elected *Seanad* 'could hardly be more pointed'.[403]

300. EU budgetary rules have constitutional status by virtue of the operation of Article 29.4.6° which places matters which are required by virtue of Ireland's EU membership in a position of superiority to all Irish law, including constitutional law. Accordingly, a number of EU budgetary and taxation rules (like the EU budgetary deficit rules for example) enjoy the force of law in Ireland and can greatly impact the public finance and taxation systems. The Thirtieth Amendment, which incorporated the Fiscal Stability Treaty, (although not strictly EU law), imposed further restraints on the Irish Government when it came to budgetary policy and taxation.

301. The office of the Comptroller and Auditor General is established by Article 33.[404] The office is an independent office and the Comptroller is excluded from being a member of the *Oireachtas*. The Comptroller's office is responsible for the payment of all disbursements by the State but perhaps more crucially the Comptroller is responsible for the auditing of 'all accounts of moneys administered by or under the authority of the *Oireachtas*'. The details of the precise requirements are determined by legislation, but the main aim of the audit is to ensure that all accounts presented by the various State bodies and entities (under the remit of the office) are a true and accurate reflection of their present fiscal position. The Auditor is also charged with ensuring that the State is getting value for money and that the resources of the State are efficiently utilized.

403. Casey (n. 84) 123.
404. *See* para. 169.

Chapter 3. Emergency Powers

302. Bunreacht na hÉireann does not have a separate article dealing with emergency powers; instead, Article 28, which deals with the Government contains a section on this. The relevant provision, Article 28.3.3°, does not bestow any additional powers on the Government but rather it allows the *Oireachtas* to vest extra powers in the Government. The provision reads as follows:

> Nothing in this Constitution other than Article 15.5.2° shall be invoked to invalidate any law enacted by the Oireachtas which is expressed to be for the purpose of securing the public safety and the preservation of the State in time of war or armed rebellion, or to nullify any act done or purporting to be done in time of war or armed rebellion in pursuance of any such law. In this subsection 'time of war' includes a time when there is taking place an armed conflict in which the State is not a participant but in respect of which each of the Houses of the Oireachtas shall have resolved that, arising out of such armed conflict, a national emergency exists affecting the vital interests of the State and 'time of war or armed rebellion' includes such time after the termination of any war, or of any such armed conflict as aforesaid, or of an armed rebellion, as may elapse until each of the Houses of the Oireachtas shall have resolved that the national emergency occasioned by such) war, armed conflict, or armed rebellion has ceased to exist.

303. Substantial power is thereby granted to the *Oireachtas* to legislate without limits, as long as the instrument is expressed to be for the specified purposes. This means that constitutional safeguards (such as fundamental rights) can be suspended and the power of the courts to review legislation can be withdrawn, subject to the sole proviso in Article 15.5.2° that any such emergency legislation cannot purport to introduce the death penalty.

304. The case of *Re Article 26 and the Emergency Powers Bill 1967*[405] clarified that Article 28.3.3° envisages two types of emergency legislation. The first is legislation designed for a time of war or armed rebellion, which, it was held does not require resolutions from the *Oireachtas* declaring a national emergency in order for Article 28.3.3° to apply; this type of legislation can be enacted if the war or armed rebellion was imminent and would come into operation when the event occurred. The second type of legislation is that which is designed to cope with an emergency brought about by an external armed rebellion. This type of legislation requires resolutions to be passed by the *Oireachtas* in order to benefit from the protection in Article 28.3.3°.

305. Despite the fact that Article 28.3.3° requires specific conditions in order to declare a state of emergency – war, armed rebellion or armed conflict – Ireland experienced a perpetual state of emergency from the outbreak of World War II on 2 September 1939 until February 1995 after an IRA[406] ceasefire was declared in Northern

405. [1977] IR 159.
406. An armed movement dedicated to Irish republicanism and a united Ireland. They were involved in a campaign of violence in the North of Ireland until the peace process in the 1990s.

Ireland and the emergency was terminated. This period involved two declarations of emergency. The first state of emergency was not repealed until 1976. However, The Emergency Powers Act, which ushered in the first state of emergency in 1939, had already lapsed in 1946 and no further emergency legislation had been passed. Following the repeal of the state of emergency in 1976, a new state of emergency was immediately declared as a result of the armed conflict taking place in the North of Ireland. The decision to declare a second state of emergency was triggered by explosions at the Special Criminal Court in Dublin on July 15 1976 and the murder of the British Ambassador, Christopher Ewart-Biggs, on July 21 1976.[407] The Emergency Powers Act 1976 was then passed. It was identical to the provisions of section 30 of the 1939 Act, apart from the fact that it permitted the *Gardaí* to detain suspects for a period of up to seven days prior to charging them. Before the Act was passed, it had been referred by the President to the Supreme Court under Article 26 for an adjudication as to its constitutionality and, although the Court upheld the Bill, it did so only the basis that the measure was immune from constitutional scrutiny for as long as the emergency resolutions were in place. The court reserved 'for future consideration the question whether the Courts have jurisdiction to review such resolutions.' The 1976 Act was not renewed by the Government in 1977 despite the fact that it could have been reactivated by executive order at any time so long as the Article 28.3.3° resolutions of 1976 remained in force.

306. Article 28.3.2° also empowers the executive to take all necessary steps to secure the safety of the State in case of actual invasion. This Article has never been relied upon.

307. The 1996 Constitution Review Group, which was established to make recommendations on reform of the Constitution, has advised that a state of emergency should be limited to a period of three years only (with an annual review thereafter) and that the Constitution should specify certain non-derogable rights, that the State cannot depart from, even during periods of emergency, so as to conform to Article 15 of the European Convention of Human Rights. It also recommended that the second and all subsequent references to 'war' contained in Article 28.3 be extended to include 'or other armed conflict' in order to prevent the Government from participating in an external conflict without the consent of the *Dáil.*

308. Article 40.4.5 contains a further emergency provision. It provides that nothing in Article 40.4 (the *habeas corpus* provision) may be invoked to prohibit, control or interfere with any act of the Defence Forces during the existence of a state of war or armed rebellion. Casey has argued that this is to be read together with Article 38.4.1°, which allows for the establishment of military tribunals to deal with a state of war or armed rebellion.[408] This would mean that a person detained pending trial by such a tribunal would not be permitted to challenge their detention by *habeas corpus.* Although, it would be for the courts to say whether the state or war or armed rebellion actually exists and thus determine the legitimacy of the tribunals.

407. For more on this *see* Alan Greene, 'The Historical Evolution of Article 28.3.3° of The Irish Constitution' (2012), 47(1) The Irish Jurist 117.
408. Casey (n. 84) 187.

Chapter 4. Relationship Between Church and State

309. As Professor Casey has stated:

> In Ireland the question of Church and State has been essentially a matter of politics rather than law. That is, it has surfaced only rarely in the courts and its central concern has been the influence of the majority Roman Catholic Church on certain issues of public policy – censorship of publications, education and, especially, family matters being among them.[409]

Around the time of the drafting of Bunreacht na hÉireann, the Catholic Church exercised immense influence on Irish life. It is well known that members of the Catholic Church were consulted and even made submissions during the drafting process. It seems that the Church wished to ensure that its values, rather than any modern secular ideas, would be enshrined in the new document. It has also been suggested that Ireland was seen by the Vatican as a potential model Catholic State in 1937 and the Church sought to bring this about.[410]

310. Originally, Article 44 on respect for religion contained two additional clauses:

> 2. The State recognizes the special position of the Holy Catholic Apostolic and Roman Church as the guardian of the Faith professed by the great majority of the citizens.

> 3. The State also recognizes the Church of Ireland, the Presbyterian Church in Ireland, the Methodist Church in Ireland, the Religious Society of Friends in Ireland, as well as the Jewish Congregations and the other religious denominations existing in Ireland at the date of the coming into operation of this Constitution.

During the *Oireachtas* debates on these provisions, the *Taoiseach* of the time and architect of the Constitution, Eamon de Valera, hinted that the 'special position' clause was a compromise, as there had been earlier proposals which would have given exclusive recognition to the Catholic Church. While there was very little opposition at the time, eventually it was recognized that these provisions were problematic and they were deleted in 1972 by the Fifth Amendment.[411]

311. In the early years of the Irish State, there was, generally speaking, a strong consensus between Church and State but from the 1960s and 70s, tensions began to arise with the spread of more liberal ideas and calls to legalize contraception and divorce. Recent years have seen a more stark separation between Church and State policy, as demonstrated by the recent Amendment to the Constitution which provided

409. Casey (n. 84) 687.
410. *See* Keogh in Litton (n. 8) and Keogh (n. 8).
411. Further Reading: Hogan (n. 8); Whyte (n. 8).

for marriage equality. However, as noted earlier[412] the vast majority of primary schools in the State are still under the patronage and ownership of the Catholic Church – something which has caused controversy in recent years and calls have been made for the divestment of these schools.

412. *See* para. 263.

Chapter 5. The Irish Language

312. According to the most recent census data,[413] the Irish language is notionally spoken by 1.77 million people who answered 'yes' to the question 'can you speak Irish?' This represented a 7% increase on the previous census and roughly equates to 41.4% of all census respondents. This figure is widely accepted to be hugely misrepresentative of the actual number of functional Irish speakers given that it takes account of school goers who undergo mandatory Irish language classes.[414] Those who typically answer yes usually (for a variety of reasons) tend to lack any level of Irish beyond the most basic phrases. The manner in which the census question was put to the public was also most unhelpful as no real evidentiary assessment of the level of Irish spoken by the respondent was requested.

313. More helpfully, the census does include a question on the frequency of the use of the Irish language outside of the education system. 77,185 respondents that were questioned replied that they use the Irish language everyday outside of the education system (an increase of 5,037 speakers since the previous census), which represents a figure which can be more accurately relied upon when asserting the functional number of Irish speakers currently active in contemporary Ireland. A further 110,642 Irish speakers claimed that they the Irish language on a weekly basis with the rest reporting that they use the language less frequently. The census data makes it clear that the Irish language is now very much a minority language in modern Ireland. It is noteworthy that Irish has been pushed into third place in Ireland with Polish which is currently being spoken by 119,562 respondents. It is within this linguistic context that the Irish language now finds itself, despite the higher constitutional status which was granted to it by the law.

314. The Irish language was first given constitutional recognition in Article 4 of the 1922 Free State Constitution, which recognized it as the 'national language', of equal standing to the English language. The position of the Irish language was further strengthened with the adoption of the 1937 Constitution which, in Article 8.1, declared that Irish was the first 'official' and national language. Article 8.2 goes on to state that English is 'recognized' as an official second language however.

315. The Irish-language versions of Articles 8.1 and 8.2 evidence some of the differences which can exist between the language versions of the Irish Constitution. The Irish text of Article 8.1 uses the expression '*príomh*' which loosely translates as primary. Such reference to the Irish language suggests a degree of primacy over the English language which appears to vest a greater status to the Irish language than that which the English text confers upon it. However the full legal ramifications of this linguistic distinction remain to be fully explored and teased out in court. The Report of the Constitutional Review Group has suggested that the designation of Irish as the national and first official language is in their view of 'little practical significance'.[415]

413. Central Statistics Office, *This Is Ireland Highlights from Census 2011, Part 1* (Stationery Office 2012) 40.

414. In spite of this mandatory Irish language education 30.9% of those aged between 10 – 19 report being unable to speak Irish at all.

415. The Constitutional Review Group (n. 233) 11.

316. Perhaps the treatment that Article 8.2 gets in the Irish text is of even more significance and interest.[416] Whilst the English text uses the word 'recognized', the Irish text offers the expression '*glactar leis*'. This phrase is more accurately translated as 'accepted as', which would seem to denote a status of grudging recognition. In other Articles of the Constitution where the English word 'recognized' is used it is usually reflected in the Irish text by the word '*admhaíonn*' which would more closely reflect the word 'recognized'. The reason for the divergence in this Article is not clear, but the plain purport of the words involved suggests that '*glactar*' should be construed as being lower in status than the word 'recognized' in the English text, although there has been little legal examination of this position and it is possible that such terminology was simply used for nationalistic or political reasons. The second element of Article 8.2 worthy of inspection is the use of the term '*Sacs-Bhéarla*' to represent the word 'English'. In the 1922 Constitution, subsequent legislation and contemporary use the Irish word '*Béarla*' is employed when referring to the English language, but in this instance the term '*Sacs*' or 'Sax' precedes it. In doing so, the drafters made an emphatic case that the English language ought to be treated as the language of the Saxon foreigner rather than as the language of the Irish people. The political significance of such a term cannot be overlooked, particularly when the 1937 Constitution was attempting to sever all of the ties with the United Kingdom that had been enshrined in the 1922 Constitution.[417] However, as Geoghegan J argued in *Ó Beoláin v. Fahy*[418] such semantic provisions amount to little more than rhetoric and have no particular legal significance.

317. Article 25.5.4° of the Constitution gives the Irish language a special legal significance when it comes to interpreting the text of the Constitution. Article 25.5.4° demands that where a conflict arises between the texts of the English and Irish versions of the Constitution, the text that is drafted in the Irish language must prevail. The theory that the Constitution was drafted in English and then subsequently translated into Irish was long considered fact however it is now generally accepted that both versions of the Constitution were drafted in and around the same time, allowing for certain steps to be taken to increase the clarity of both texts.[419]

318. In many cases, ambiguities in one text are resolved when the reader embraces the other. The classic example is Article 12.4.1° on the eligibility for the presidency. The English text states that any person who has reached their 35th year may take office (which would include someone who was 34 years of age, which one imagines was not the original intention of the drafters when they stipulated the provision) while the Irish text clearly establishes that a person must have attained their 35th year (i.e. they must be 35 or older) in order to take office.

319. Despite the opportunities that are offered by having the Irish text take precedence over the English text (particularly in those instances where the English text is unsatisfactory) no less a scholar than Ireland's most celebrated constitutional lawyer Prof J.M. Kelly has described Article 25.5.4° as something of an 'irrational irritant' that creates a 'situation [which is] pregnant with annoyance and timewasting

416. The Irish text reads 'Glactar leis an Sacs-Bhéarla mar theanga oifigiúil eile.' while the English text reads 'The English language is recognised as a second official language.'
417. *See* para. 9.
418. Ó Beoláin (n. 197).
419. *See generally* All-Party Oireachtas Committee on the Constitution (n. 29).

for the Courts'.[420] Kelly's views are possibly influenced by the generally-accepted position of his time that the Irish version was a mere translation of the English version. The most satisfactory position with regards to interpreting both texts is perhaps best described as constructive and complementary. As Budd J noted in *O'Donovan v. Attorney General*:

> Both texts of the Constitution are authoritative. It is not to be thought that those who framed or enacted the Constitution would knowingly do anything so absurd as to frame or enact texts with different meanings in parts. It could only happen by inadvertence…if in fact the words used are not in form really found to correspond the Irish text must prevail.[421]

320. In many of the most high-profile constitutional cases the Courts have turned to the Irish text in order to correctly interpret the meaning of a particular provision of the Constitution.[422] Having two linguistic versions of the text has tended to aid interpretation in these cases rather than add an additional barrier to finding the correct interpretation.

321. Speakers of the Irish language have had certain recognition of their rights to use the language and to engage with the State through the medium of Irish. While the Irish language had no legal status in Ireland prior to independence, since 1922 speakers of Irish have had their rights recognized by virtue of the constitutional status that has been conferred upon the language. The first prominent recognition of Irish language rights in Ireland occurred in *Attorney General v. Joyce and Walsh*,[423] where Kennedy CJ held that the text of the Constitution conferred what he termed a 'double right' (both natural and constitutional) to Irish speakers who wished to engage with the State and in the Courts through the medium of Irish. A significant conflict between theory and practice developed when it came to language rights in Ireland as speakers of Irish often had to resort to legal actions to spur the State into providing its basic services and engagement through the medium of Irish.

322. The impact of language rights was best illustrated in the majority judgment of the Court in *Ó Beoláin v. Fahy*[424] where the Court gave a warning to the State that the continued failure to vindicate the rights of Irish speakers and the ongoing failure of the State to fulfil its constitutional obligations towards the Irish language could result in criminal prosecutions being dismissed. The impact and ramifications of this judgment were profound; it spurred the State on to a more progressive engagement with the Irish language and a more proactive vindication of Irish language rights in general. State action took the form of the passing of The Official Languages Act, 2003 which both codified the State's constitutional language obligations and created an

420. John Maurice Kelly, 'The Irish Text of the Constitution' (1966) Irish Student Law Review 7, 10.
421. [1961] IR 114 117.
422. Examples include; *Doherty v. Government of Ireland* [2010] IEHC 369; *Roche v. Roche* [2009] IESC 82; *Sinnott v. Ireland* [2001] IESC 63; *Attorney General v. X* (n. 148).
423. [1929] IR 526 – Although this case concerned the 1922 Constitution its findings have been approved in subsequent case law concerning the 1937 Constitution.
424. *Ó Beoláin* (n. 197).

official language ombudsman known as the *Coimisinéir Teanga*. The State also engaged proactively with European Union mechanisms, and in 2007, the Irish language was declared a full official EU language, which meant that it is now, for the very first time, co-equal in status with all of the other official EU languages.

Chapter 6. The Constitutional Convention

323. The Convention on the Constitution, more commonly referred to as the Constitutional Convention, was established by Resolution of both Houses of the *Oireachtas* to consider and make recommendations on a number of topics as possible future amendments to the Constitution. There had been a number of reports considering constitutional reform in the past: the 1967 Committee on the Constitution which involved a mix of TDs and Senators who recommended various reforms to the Constitution; the Constitution Review Group which was an expert group that produced its report in 1996 and the All-party *Oireachtas* Committee on the Constitution which produced a number of reports on various aspects of the Constitution from 1997 to 2006. While many recommendations for reform were put forward, very few were acted upon.

324. However, in 2012, for the first time, ordinary Irish citizens were involved in making recommendations for reform. The Convention comprised 100 people, representative of Irish society and parliamentarians from the whole island of Ireland, with an independent Chairman. Besides the chairman, the Convention membership included twenty-nine members of the *Oireachtas*, four representatives from Northern Irish political parties and sixty-six randomly selected Irish citizens. While the citizen members were randomly selected by a polling company using the electoral register, they were also chosen in a manner so as to be representative of Irish society as a whole and were balanced in terms of gender, age, region, etc.

325. The agenda set for the convention was to consider the following topics:

(1) reducing the presidential term of office from seven to five years and aligning it with the scheduling of local and European elections;
(2) reducing the minimum voting age from 18 to 17 years of age;
(3) reviewing the *Dáil* electoral system;
(4) giving Irish citizens resident outside the State the right to vote in Irish presidential elections at Irish embassies, or in some other manner which would be prescribed by law;
(5) providing for same-sex marriage;
(6) amending the constitutional clause on the role of women in the home and encouraging greater participation of women in public life;
(7) increasing the participation of women in politics;
(8) removing the offence of blasphemy from the Constitution; and
(9) following completion of the above reports, such other relevant constitutional amendments that may be recommended by the Convention.

The 'other relevant' areas considered by the Convention were *Dáil* reform and economic, social and cultural rights.

326. The establishment of the Convention was criticized by many at the outset who believed it was simply a way for the Government to wash its hands of issues related to constitutional reform which they did not want to engage with and also because many of the issues given to the Convention to consider were effectively non-issues or at least issues which had not been flagged as being in dire need of reform. In contrast there were other key subjects, such as abortion and the Eighth Amendment, which were not included on the agenda.

327. Whatever the intention of the Government in establishing the Convention, it is widely regarded as having been a success. The Convention met over ten weekends. Each meeting had three components: a presentation by experts of papers which had been circulated in advance; a debate between groups advocating on either side of the issue; and a number of roundtable discussions involving facilitators and note-takers. On Sunday morning the members reconsidered the discussions of the previous day and voted by ballot paper on the details of the debate.

328. The Convention produced nine reports containing recommendations. Although the Government was required to respond officially to all of the reports within four months, this deadline was missed for the fourth and subsequent reports. Therefore no formal response was made to the remaining reports by the time the *Dáil* adjourned for its summer recess on 17 July 2014. The delayed response to these reports was not given until 14 January 2016. Given the enthusiasm of Convention members and the interest that the Convention process had garnered in both the media and the public, the lack of genuine engagement from the Government following the issuing of these reports was somewhat disappointing. However, the Government did fulfil its promise to present two of the Convention issues to the people in a referendum – the question of lowering the age of eligibility for the presidency and the question of clarifying the definition of marriage in the Constitution (to include same-sex marriage). While the people were not in favour of the first proposal, they voted 62% in favour of the second. Vague assurances have been made to put some of the other issues to a referendum in the future, while some of the proposals on *Dáil* reform were implemented without the need for constitutional change.

329. A similar Citizen's Assembly was established in October 2016 by the Government in order to further consider the issues around abortion and the Eighth amendment in Ireland as well as questions on fixed term parliaments, referendums, population ageing, and climate change. The Assembly is currently finalizing its report on the Eighth amendment in which it is set to recommend to the Oireachtas the legalization of abortion in Ireland in a wide range of circumstances. It remains to be seen what effect the recommendations of the Assembly will have in terms of law reform.

Selected Bibliography

Articles

Laura Cahillane, 'Ireland's System for Disciplining and Removing Judges' (2015) 38 Dublin University Law Journal 55.

Laura Cahillane, 'The Prerogative and its Survival in Ireland: Dusty Antique or Positively Useful?' (2010) 1(2) IJLS 1.

Alpha Connolly, 'Implications of the ECHR Act 2003' (2004) 98 (7) LSG 7.

Alan Greene, 'The Historical Evolution of Article 28.3.3° of The Irish Constitution' (2012), 47(1) The Irish Jurist 117.

Gerard Hogan, 'Law and Religion: Church-State Relations in Ireland from Independence to the Present Day' (1987) 35 AJCL 47.

Gerard Hogan, 'Unenumerated Personal Rights: Ryan's Case Re-evaluated' (1990-92) Irish Jurist 95.

Aileen Kavanagh, 'The quest for legitimacy in constitutional interpretation' (1997) 32 Irish Jurist 195.

John Maurice Kelly, 'The Irish Text of the Constitution' (1966) Irish Student Law Review 7.

Thomas Mohr, 'Law Without Loyalty – The Abolition of the Irish Appeal to the Privy Council' (2002) Irish Jurist 187.

David Gwynn Morgan, '"Judicial-o-centric" separation of powers on the wane?' (2004) 39 Irish Jurist 142

David Gwynn Morgan, 'Selection of Superior Judges' (2004) 22 I.L.T. 42

Bláthna Ruane, 'Reflections on Procedural Rights in Constitutional Referenda' (2012) 47(2) Irish Jurist 1.

Jonothan Tomkin, 'Implementing Community Legislation into National Law' (2004) Judicial Studies Institute Journal Volume 4 No. 2 130.

Books

Raymond Byrne and Paul McCutcheon, *The Irish Legal System* (4th edn, Butterworths, 2001).

Laura Cahillane, *Drafting the Irish Free State Constitution* (MUP, 2016).

Selected Bibliography

Eoin Carolan and Oran Doyle (eds), *The Irish Constitution: Governance and Values* (Thomson Round Hall, 2008).

James Casey, *Constitutional Law in Ireland* (3rd edn, Round Hall, 2000).

Micheál Cearúil, *Bunreacht na hÉireann: A Study of the Irish Text* (The Stationery Office, 1999).

Oran Doyle, *Constitutional Law: Text, Cases and Materials* (Clarus Press, 2008).

Michael Forde and David Leonard, *Constitutional Law of Ireland* (3rd edn, Bloomsbury, 2013).

Tom Hesketh, *The Second Partitioning of Ireland: The Abortion Referendum of 1983* (Branndsma Books, 1990).

Gerard Hogan and Gerry Whyte, *JM Kelly: The Irish Constitution* (Butterworths Dublin, 2003).

David Gwynn Morgan, *The Separation of Powers in the Irish Constitution* (Round Hall, 1997).

David Gwynn Morgan, *Constitutional Law of Ireland* (2nd edn, Round Hall, 1990).

David Gwynn Morgan, *A Judgment Too Far? Judicial Activism and the Constitution* (Cork University Press, 2001).

Conor O'Mahony, *Educational Rights in Irish Law* (Thomson Round Hall, 2006).

James O'Reilly (ed.), *Human Rights and Constitutional Law* (Thomson Round Hall, 1992).

Jennifer Schweppe (ed.), *The Unborn Child, Article 40.3.3° and Abortion in Ireland: Twenty-Five Years of Protection?* (Liffey Press, 2008).

John Henry Whyte, *Church and State in Modern Ireland 1923-1979* (2nd edn, Gill & Macmillan Dublin, 1980).

The Constitutional Review Group, *Report of the Constitution Review Group* (Stationery Office, 1996).

Index

The numbers here refer to paragraph numbers.

Index

www.ingramcontent.com/pod-product-compliance
Lightning Source LLC
Chambersburg PA
CBHW071349230926
51846CB00002B/488
* 9 7 8 9 0 4 1 1 9 3 0 9 4 *